Industrialization and Gender Inequality

by

Louise A. Tilly

With a Foreword by Michael Adas, Series Editor

D1301665

American Historical Association
400 A Street SE
Washington, D.C., 20003-3889

Louise A. Tilly is professor of history and sociology at the New School for Social Research and chair of its Committee on Historical Studies. She is past president of the American Historical Association. Her work focuses on the small-scale effects of large-scale social change in concrete historical settings, especially in France and Italy since 1800, and with emphases on gender and class. She has written extensively and published in a wide range of journals, books, papers, reviews, and symposia.

Series Editor: Michael Adas
Pamphlets Production Editor: Roxanne Myers Spencer

This essay originally appeared in *Islamic & European Expansion: The Forging of a Global Order*, published by Temple University Press in the series *Critical Perspectives on the Past*, edited by Susan Porter Benson, Stephen Brier, and Roy Rosenzweig. Copyright © 1993 Temple University.

ISBN: 0-87229-072-7.
This edition published by the American Historical Association.
Printed in the United States of America.

Contents

Essays in Global and Comparative History

Foreword

Given the previously rather peripheral position of global and comparative history in the discipline, the growth of interest in these fields over the past three decades or so has been truly remarkable. The appearance of numerous works by prominent scholars on transcultural interaction and on variations in social systems and political economies, the great proliferation at both the college and secondary-school level of courses on world history and numerous textbooks with which to teach them, and the formation in recent years of the World History Association, an affiliate of the American Historical Association, all testify to the increasing importance of global and comparative scholarship and teaching within the historical profession. In some ways these developments represent a revival, for world or cross-cultural history is as ancient as Herodotus, and it enjoyed particular favor among Western intellectuals from the eighteenth to the early twentieth centuries. But challenges to the grand designs or underlying "laws" that writers like Spengler or Toynbee discerned in human history, as well as an increasing emphasis on area specialization within the discipline as a whole, led to doubts about the feasibility or even the advisability of attempting to generalize across vast swaths of time and space. In scholarship, world history came to be seen as a pastime for dilettantes or popularists; in teaching, it was increasingly equated with unfocused social studies courses at the secondary-school level.

Though the current interest in global history reflects a continuing fascination with the broad patterns of human development across cultures that were the focus for earlier works on world history, the "new" global or world history differs in fundamental ways from its predecessors. Writers of the new global history are less concerned with comprehensiveness or with providing a total chronology of human events. Their works tend to be thematically focused on recurring processes like war and colonization or on cross-cultural patterns like the spread of disease, technology, and trading networks. Their works are often more consciously and systematically comparative than the studies of earlier world historians. Partly because the research of area specialists has provided today's scholars with a good deal more data than was available to earlier writers, the best recent works on global history also display a far greater sensitivity than the more comprehensive world surveys to cultural nuances and the intricacies of the internal histories of the societies they cover. In addition, few practitioners of the new global history see their task as one of establishing universal "laws" or of identifying an overall teleological meaning in human development. Their main concerns are the study of recurring processes and the dynamics and effects of cross-cultural interaction. Depending on their original area orientation, global and comparative historians adopt these approaches because they see them as the most effective way of bringing the experience of the "people without history" into the mainstream of teaching and scholarship, of relating the development of Europe to that of the rest of the world, or of challenging the misleading myth of exceptionalism that has dominated so much of the work on the history of the United States.

This series of essays is intended to provide an introduction to the new world history. Each pamphlet explores some of the interpretations and understandings that have resulted from crosscultural and comparative historical studies undertaken in the past three or four decades. The pamphlets are designed to assist both college and secondary-school teachers who are engaged in teaching courses on world history or courses with a comparative format. Each essay is authored by an expert on the time period or process in question. Though brief lists or works that teachers might consult for more detailed information on the topic covered are included in each of the pamphlets, the essays are not intended to be bibliographic surveys. Their central aim is to provide teachers facing the formidable task of preparing courses that are global or cross-cultural in scope with a sense of some of the issues that have been of interest to scholars working in these areas in recent decades. The essays deal with specific findings and the debates these have often generated, as well as broad patterns that cross-cultural study has revealed and their implications for the history of specific societies. Although all of the essays are thematically oriented, some are organized around particular historical eras like the age of Islamic expansion or the decades of industrialization, while others are focused on key topics like slavery or revolution. Because there are many approaches to global history, these essays vary in format and content, from ones that are argumentative and highly interpretive to others that concentrate on giving an overview of major patterns or processes in global development. Each essay, however, suggests some of the most effective ways of dealing with the topic or the era covered, given the current state of our knowledge. In recognition of the quincentenary of Columbus's "discovery" of the Americas, the series begins with an essay on the impact of the processes set in motion by his voyages. Subsequent pamphlets cover topics and time periods from the era of early European overseas expansion to the present and then from the era of expansion back to the time of the Neolithic Revolution.

Michael Adas, Series Editor
Professor of History
Rutgers University

Industrialization and Gender Inequality

LOUISE A. TILLY

There is no hardship in women working for a living,
the hardship lies in not getting a living
when they work for it.
—Clara Collet

To what extent did industrialization reduce gender inequality? This blunt and simple question is a basic one in women's history. As Clara Collet suggests, there is no simple answer.[1] Jeffrey Williamson's econometric study of male earnings and income inequality in the British Industrial Revolution finds that during the century from 1760 to 1860, excepting the period of war with revolutionary and Napoleonic France, inequality among men in Britain rose. He sums up: "The income shares at the top rose, the shares at the bottom fell, the relative pay of the unskilled deteriorated, the premium on skills increased, and the earnings distribution widened." In the 1830s and after, however, the real wages of the average (male) worker rose.[2] Williamson's ingenuity in uncovering sources that can be quantified for analysis is matched by that of Claudia Goldin, who has analyzed U.S. wage data for men and women from 1815 to the present, focusing on the ratio of female to male earnings. Although this earnings ratio (for full-time workers) narrowed substantially with the new availability of manufacturing jobs in addition to agricultural ones in the early nineteenth century, and a similar narrowing occurred with the initial opening up of clerical jobs, there has been no sustained improvement for decades.[3] Both Williamson and Goldin produce valuable and interesting comparisons by simplifying the question to the point where relatively reliable evidence over long periods can be found and compared among groups and over time.

For many historians, these econometric analyses leave out too much.[4] Women's historians have excelled in studies of work, gender relations in the household, and politics that draw a less precise, more nuanced, and complex picture. Overall trends in gender inequality are exceedingly diffi-

1

cult to determine not only because any aggregate measure of the phenomenon must combine many dimensions but also because the respective importance of specific forms of gender inequality varies over space and time. In the face of these daunting problems, I have chosen to address the extent to which *forms* of gender inequality have varied with different political and economic conditions, rather than absolute levels or trends. The hypothesis underlying the cross-national comparisons presented here is that over long periods, political economic factors—markets, trade, technology, the organization of production and social reproduction (in particular, the sex division of labor in the workplace and the home), national and local policies—lie behind variations in gender relations. Modifications in these arenas, shaping and interacting with demographic processes and history (including cultural practices, ideologies, and social movements), change opportunities for communities, classes, families, and individuals to make their living, acquire resources, cope with and control their lives.[5] This essay compares recent historical research about these matters (with emphasis on the sex division of labor), puts forward the outlines of a synthesis, and proposes an agenda for continuing historical research.

The Debate on the Industrial Revolution and Women

Writing in the 1920s, Ivy Pinchbeck—the first modern historian who addressed the central question of the effect of the Industrial Revolution on women's lives—was of two minds. Rejecting any preindustrial golden age, she argued that although women workers' conditions in the early factories were bad, they were no worse than those in nonmechanized jobs (dressmaking, for example) done in households, in which they were exploited by greedy middlemen. Factories meant better wages and a higher standard of living. Married women (the majority of whom did not earn wages regularly) were subjected to greater inequality—she admitted—than wives had been when they contributed directly to family income. This was not all bad, Pinchbeck wrote, for the Industrial Revolution "led to the assumption that men's wages should be paid on a family basis, and prepared the way for the more modern conception that in the rearing of children and in homemaking, the married woman makes an adequate economic contribution." Middle-class women, observing women workers' greater social and economic independence, Pinchbeck continued, became conscious of their own rights and demanded education and jobs for themselves.[6]

In the past twenty years or so the histories of women, family, and gender have become flourishing fields, and the relationship of industrial transformation and gender inequality a topic of renewed interest. Contemporary historians, writing in a period when feminists question gender relations in both public and domestic spheres, have not hesitated to historicize the family as well as the workplace. What is the current state of the question?

Not surprisingly, historians are still divided between optimists and pessimists about the effects of industrialization on gender inequality.[7]

Edward Shorter, a representative optimist, concerned primarily with men's and women's relations within the family, argues that a shift toward sex equality occurred about the middle of the eighteenth century. He writes of the "surge of sentiment"—linked with "laissez-faire marketplace organization, capitalist production, and the beginnings of proletarianization" that revolutionized family relations in western Europe. The "First Sexual Revolution," is revealed, he asserts, by increased illegitimacy rates in many parts of Europe. Access to wage-earning jobs, in particular those made newly available by industrialization, made women more conscious of themselves as individuals and ready to seek sexual pleasure.[8]

An exemplary pessimist is Sonya Rose, who addresses the failure of women's wage earning to reduce gender inequality in the workplace or the family. In her studies of the East Midlands hosiery industry, Rose argues for the interdependence of patriarchal and capitalist gender relations: When hosiery making moved to the factory and paid individual wages to men and women who had worked together cooperatively in household production, conflict between workers of the two sexes became more salient. The capitalists' solution was segregated jobs, with lower wages for women, and supervisory posts for some men. Rose concludes that both workers and their employers acted out of the belief that women's proper role was that of wife and mother and in doing so reinforced that ideology.[9]

There are still lacunae in our knowledge of the relationship of industrialization and gender relations. Nevertheless, enough evidence exists to make systematic comparisons, draw some modest conclusions about variation in the forms of inequality, and suggest an agenda for continuing research.

That is the goal of this essay.[10]

A Comparative Framework for Studying Gender Inequality

The task is to compare both patterns of large-scale structural change and social groups at the micro level, seeking regularities in variation of the forms of gender inequality as they are articulated with the process of industrialization.[11] Such comparisons must take history seriously, examining the ways in which what happens at one point in time may constrain what comes after, setting the conditions for developments in a second period.

Gender is defined as the social organization of relations between the sexes. Gender inequality is the structured pattern of gender asymmetries in well-being, as measured by capabilities. Here I adopt the conceptualization of Amartya Sen, who writes that "there is a good case for judging individual well-being, neither in terms of commodities consumed nor in terms of the mental metric of utilities, but in terms of the 'capabilities' of persons. This is the perspective of 'freedom' in the *positive* sense: who can *do* what."[12] The capabilities approach, he argues, can take account of personal characteristics such as sex and age and not simply the resources to which individuals may have access.

Sen has also proposed a dynamic way of conceptualizing the relationship between the sex division of labor in the household and that in the economy. He sees family as a site of cooperative conflict in which bargaining or negotiation is an ongoing process. Family bargaining involves cooperation and conflict because interdependency in the household "makes it fruitful for the different parties to cooperate, but the particular pattern of division of fruits that emerges from such cooperation reflects the 'bargaining powers' of the respective parties." Men's wages earned outside the household undergirded their stronger bargaining power early on; such an advantage could, following Sen, "lead to a correspondingly more favorable cooperative outcome for the men." The advantage gained at one point in time would lead to a stronger position in the next period of bargaining: "Certain 'traditional' arrangements may emerge, e.g., women doing housework and being able to take up outside work *only if* it is additional. These inequalities may solidify over time."[13]

Gender inequality increases when the difference between male and female capabilities increases, and vice versa. (Thus it is critical to distinguish changes that benefit men and women—of a given social group in a specified time and place—equally and those that reduce or increase inequality between them.) I examine capabilities in both domestic and public spheres, in production and reproduction (understood broadly as both physical and social), and in politics. Within arenas, national states, and time periods, I stress variation by class and gender (and where applicable, by race), and seek to show its systematic character.[14]

The English Case: The First Industrial Revolution

The concept of an Industrial Revolution has been challenged by economic and social historians, as Peter Stearns has shown.[15] I continue to use the words *Industrial Revolution* to describe industrialization in England because it was first, and because it was a unique event in its time.

Most of the population in seventeenth-century Britain lived in rural areas and worked in agriculture. Fertility and mortality rates were both high, but population growth was slow because of late marriage, a high degree of nonmarriage (and little reproduction outside marriage), and intermittent peaks of crisis mortality. Rural households produced most of the articles needed in their daily life (food, cloth and clothing, furniture, vessels for cooking and eating) with the help of tools often made by specialists. A sex division of labor existed within these households, but high levels of mortality and the small size of households meant that there were not always individuals of the requisite age and sex to perform a given task; hence there was flexibility in the division of labor.

As the manorial system and its feudal underpinnings broke up, parcels of land were assembled into large farms, rented and directed by farmers employing wage labor. They increased productivity by economies of scale and innovation in crop mix and rotation. Greater specialization in some occupations meant declining flexibility in tasks performed and fewer skills among nonspecialists, including women. Long before the conventional dating of the Industrial Revolution (1760–1860), then, sex and gender had become determinants of who would do a job, not capability. Women's jobs already had familiar characteristics: many fewer types, limited opportunities for advancement or the development of skill, lower pay than male jobs.[16]

Early modern urban economies were more highly differentiated centers of commerce and consumer production, with craft workers usually organized in guilds. Diverse urban populations were linked by the exchange of goods, services, and cash. There too, productive units were small, often households. Construction, food production, and cloth and garment making were all oriented to local demand. Servants (who provided personal service but often participated as well in household production for exchange) were a large proportion of urban workers; there were also wage earners outside the guild system whose numbers increased over the centuries. Although there were some women's guilds, and a woman could inherit her husband's guild mastership, there was a clear sex division of labor in early modern cities, with most women engaged predominantly in petty trading, sewing, domestic, or menial waged labor.[17]

By the end of the seventeenth century, capitalist organization of household production—protoindustry—was spreading outward from the cities, as merchant entrepreneurs sought profits through evading guild control of markets. According to Hans Medick, the sex division of labor in protoindustry was more flexible, task assignment less determined by gender than that in households engaged in large-scale agriculture or urban manufacturing. Capital–labor relations were less oppressive in protoindustry than in later large-scale industry, and households were charged with assigning tasks among themselves; the cooperation implicit in this family economy promoted gender equality, he believes. Others show a residual rigidity in the sex division of labor, however, partly a result of mothers' integral role in physical reproduction, and partly because men do not seem to have contributed to even the limited amount of housework done in the period. Thus it was that women were permitted—and often required by family need—to engage in production for exchange, while men specialized in such work and left physical and social reproduction to their wives. Household-based labor was offered to impoverished rurals; women's family responsibilities were fitted around their wage work. The availability of such work made it easier for rural people to marry young, and population grew more rapidly in many protoindustrial areas than in areas where such opportunities did not exist.[18]

Patterns of employment in British agriculture suggest proportionately increasing, and more regular, employment of males in the south and east in the eighteenth century, with only a postharvest and winter dead season. After 1750, female agricultural unemployment rose in the harvest season and after, as women's wage earning was limited to the spring season (when lower-waged tasks were performed). Gender differentiation had increased in agricultural occupations. In a parallel process, women's agricultural wages fell continuously from 1760 on, while male real wages rose or were steady until about thirty years later. In the west of England, where women were the preferred workers in dairying and pastoral agriculture, a pattern gendered in the opposite sense prevailed, with female real wages rising above male in the early nineteenth century. K.D.M. Snell argues that increased specialization of grain cultivation in the east, changing agricultural technology (the substitution of heavier harvesting tools such as scythes for the sickle), plus social variables like the decreasing age of marriage and higher fertility rates lay behind these changes. By the 1830s, there had been a substantial decline in rural women's earning capabilities. A parallel decline in women's access to apprenticeship occurred in the eighteenth century. There was no "golden age" of women's work: Women were always the minority of apprentices, sometimes a very small one indeed, and they were unlikely ever to be economically independent; " 'male' trades were indeed male dominated." [19]

Changes in rural women's work opportunities sent many women to cities to seek jobs. Domestic service was the chief urban occupation open to girls and women migrating from the countryside. Such jobs were easier for rural women to get than either craft or factory jobs, for which urban connections were important. Service also provided room and board, thus avoiding the problems of finding lodging and its expense. In a Lancashire textile town in the mid-nineteenth century, live-in servants were found primarily in households with no wife or ones with young children. These households were frequently those of retailers, in which servants helped in the shop as well as doing domestic work. The typical servant was a solitary maid-of-all-work. She was likely to be young, as service was a life-cycle occupation, a way for rural women to earn an urban living before marriage. The predominantly rural origin of servants was a consequence as well of urban women's disdain for such jobs, and their alternative opportunities. As the English population urbanized in the course of the nineteenth century, the supply of servants dwindled, and the occupation started to decline proportionately.[20]

To what extent did the industrial revolutionary changes in the organization of production improve or hurt women's position as workers?

Textile manufacturing had long provided work for women. Although the new cotton-spinning machines put women hand spinners out of business, the water frames and jennies continued to provide jobs almost exclusively for women and children. The spinning mule (introduced later) required more physical strength and was more expensive to buy and maintain; it quickly became a male-operated machine, and even when more easily managed models became available, the male mule spinners' union opposed the employment of women and children. (Historians disagree about the mule spinners' motives: To what extent did they seek to exclude women and children totally; or was their opposition a tactic to achieve a shorter workday for all workers in the spinning rooms?) The factory organization of production that developed employed male cotton spinners assisted by women and children piecers, and adult cotton weavers of both sexes, assisted by child tenters. This division of labor entailed a modified family economy with factory textile jobs for persons of both sexes and different ages; in the cotton industry, "family wage" referred to wage pooling. In the late nineteenth and early twentieth centuries, cotton weaving was one of the few specialties in which wage *rates* were equal for men and women in the same occupation, married women worked on a regular basis, and women workers were likely to be union members. Indeed, these three characteristics were integrally connected.[21]

Maxine Berg shows that early technological change in the metal trades neither involved increased scale nor replaced the household workshop. In Birmingham, where small metalwares were the specialty, women and children specialized in button manufacturing; in areas where heavy industry dominated, women were nailers or chain makers, trades already degraded and poorly paid in the eighteenth century. Later, women's jobs were confined to the lighter and unskilled branches. The new technologies did not involve a sharp break, but deepened gender divisions already in place. The worsening wages and working conditions for women in the Birmingham metalware industry in the nineteenth century were consequences of decline in the industry itself and defensive capitalist cost cutting.

The subdivision of labor processes (driven by the search for efficiency) proceeded in other industries as well. Women workers were usually confined, by employers' decisions, to occupations designated as less skilled and were paid lower wages. The reorganization of the clothing industry, for example, writes Angela John, "confirmed rather than disturbed the basis of gender relations."[22]

Courtauld's, one of England's major silk manufacturers, sought to shape its workers' lives in the family as well as the workplace. In the nineteenth century, silk weaving (formerly concentrated in London) migrated to regions such as Essex, where cheap labor could be found because of structural unemployment in the woolen industry and in agriculture. There the company initiated such policies as the gender segregation of jobs, distinctive male and female mobility patterns (the former, involving a minority of workers, provided ladders for vertical mobility; the latter, affecting the majority, permitted only horizontal mobility), and various paternalistic schemes to teach orderly habits, mostly to women. When women's labor-market position improved at the end of the nineteenth century, Judith Lown argues, an alliance of capitalism and patriarchy blocked their efforts to forward their own interests. The "family wage" (one adequate to support a family) granted men workers by Courtauld's at this time tended both to reinforce patriarchy in the household and marginalize women in the workplace.[23]

In the Potteries (the six Staffordshire towns in which most English ceramic manufacturing was concentrated), innovative entrepreneurs had increased productivity organizationally, rather than through labor-saving technology, in the eighteenth century. There were jobs for men, women, and children in the potbanks. From 1861 to 1881, women (37 percent of the workforce), most of them unmarried, specialized in china painting, but some served (along with children) as assistants to skilled male turners and throwers. By 1901, 45.6 percent of ceramics workers were female, with a higher proportion of them married. Pottery couples had high marital fertility (much higher than did textile workers), as retrospectively measured in 1911. Child labor was still important in the twentieth century because of the workers' custom of subcontracting kin as helpers. In the potbanks (as in the cotton industry) the "family wage" referred to wage pooling among family members. Wives both worked for wages when needed and (as was common in all working-class families) were responsible for stretching the family's income. Women's wages were generally lower than men's, but their skill (well remunerated, relative to other women's wages) and their kin and community support networks contributed to two positive features of their lives: their relatively strong household position and high levels of union participation.[24]

The coal mining industry, providing vital fuel to factories, both grew and was transformed. Although earlier, wives and daughters had worked in the mines as members of family economies, helping male family members, by the nineteenth century this type of production had been superseded by larger-scale capitalist enterprise with a male workforce. There were very few women underground workers in the industry, but reformers called for laws to eliminate women from underground work. Abusive conditions were not addressed, nor was women's need for income; restrictive gender ideology drove women's exclusion. Exceptionally, mine owners and workers in Lancashire allied with feminist supporters of women's right to work to except the "pit brow lasses," girls and women who worked at the surface.[25]

Several studies of the effect of industrial transformation on working-class family relations and the domestic arena (which was of course thoroughly interrelated with the world of work) are especially telling in their translation of Sen's notion of family cooperative conflict into flesh and blood.

In the north of England, wives' responsibility for running the household was usually a matter of stretching inadequate wages, not "choosing" how to spend them. Wives were often obliged to pitch in to earn needed cash, through part-time "penny capitalism" (taking in washing, lodgers, or sewing, child minding, and retailing), charring, or full-time paid labor in textile factories. These women lacked developed concepts of their individual interests; their satisfaction came from performing their household tasks well and launching their children into the world of work.[26]

Interviews with Liverpuddlers about life in the 1920s and 1930s, although late for our purposes, provide another perspective on women's responsibility for the household budget. There, "deception and silences between husbands and wives—especially around financial questions—seemed imperative for ensuring household survival and marital stability." Women's labor-intensive efforts to supplement their husbands' wages were often ingenious, but their husbands simply refused to participate in money management, avoiding confrontation over the adequacy of their wage. Violence against wives was often a consequence of their contesting such an arrangement, challenging their husbands as wage earners when their own desperate efforts to stretch resources failed. Most often, the threat of violence was enough to silence wives, for they faced no less insecurity outside marriage.[27]

The emergence of a more rigid division of labor in many households, with husbands as the single wage earner, rendered wives' contribution incommensurate with that of their husbands and opened the way to its devaluation.

Fertility rates remained high among most groups in the English population through most of the nineteenth century. Mortality rates began to decline in the late eighteenth century among children and young people, ending the rough balance between births and deaths that had slowed population growth; the age of marriage fell to a low of twenty-one around 1800, increasing fertility. Earlier marriage has been attributed both to better real wages and to the availability of wages for women and children in protoindustry, booming in the period before 1800. (Since children were welcomed as workers in household production, there was little incentive for protoindustrial families to control fertility.) The 1851 census reported 1.7 million workers employed in factories, the wave of the future. Such industries as ceramics and textiles continued to employ many women and children, at least partly because of the family economy's adaptation to the factory. Protoindustry declined, and heavy industries such as railroad building and operations, metallurgy and engineering, and mining grew as a proportion of the industrial sector in the 1840s and later. Except in urban garment making, in which sweated household-based industry spread in the second half of the century, women's employment fell. Single working-class women continued to do wage work, but married women were more likely to earn in household production or part-time work, or to go in and out of the labor force in patterns shaped by local labor markets.[28]

In Britain as a whole, women's and children's monetary contributions to households declined, the age of marriage edged up, and lifetime non-marriage increased. The new conditions made fertility control a rational decision for working-class families. Couples married in 1861–69 had an average of 6.16 children; those who wed in 1890–99 had 4.13 children; and 1920–24 couples had 2.31 children. By the decade before World War I, average age at marriage was back to twenty-four, its 1700 level. Illegitimate fertility, which had risen along with legitimate fertility in the late eighteenth century, also fell in the last decades of the nineteenth. David Levine links fertility decline to changes in the organization of production and corresponding reorganization of social reproduction in the family.[29]

Another nineteenth-century demographic phenomenon relevant to gender inequality is the high female mortality rate relative to male in age groups from ten to thirty-nine years that became apparent in the late 1830s. In these age groups, rural females had *higher* death rates than urban women, who were in turn better off than urban males. By the 1870s, this age- and sex-specific pattern had begun to erode, and by 1900, it had disappeared. There were similar patterns in continental Europe and the United States. S. Ryan Johansson's explanation is that British rural girls and women were disadvantaged vis-à-vis males because of their reduced access to wage labor and declining economic value. With urbanization and better care in pregnancy and childbirth, female life expectancy improved appreciably: A woman born in 1831 could expect to live into her mid-sixties; a woman born in 1891 would live on average to her late seventies. Male life expectancy increased more slowly and remained lower than female, a pattern still evident today.[30]

In their examination of gender relations in the middle-class family and enterprise from 1780 to 1850, Leonore Davidoff and Catherine Hall argue that middle-class men were "embedded in networks of familial and female support which underpinned their rise to public prominence." Women made contributions to the family enterprise through work, contacts, and inherited capital. Because of civil disabilities, however, married women could not accumulate capital on their own account.

They voted and spoke in dissenting churches, however, and made financial contributions as well. Women's religious activity in the evangelical reform movement brought them into the public sphere at the same time that they were constrained by practices sanctioned by domestic ideologies that evangelical social commentators, many of them women, delineated.

Indeed, middle-class women themselves were committed to an "imperative moral code and the reworking of their domestic world into a proper setting for its practice." Legal, political, and social institutions subordinated women at the same time that they recognized their contribution to the family enterprise. As those businesses became larger scale, women were more and more limited (and limited themselves) to managing their large families (and forwarding their interests in private ways). The social relations that emerged with industrialism defined a middle-class male world of politics and production and a female world of domesticity; middle-class women were denied the citizenship that men earned in the period. Despite ideological and legal impediments, however, some middle-class women earned their living (however inadequate), and many were active in philanthropic causes, thus making an important—and acceptable—contribution to society and laying the groundwork for feminist activism.[31]

Increasing electoral participation by men after the Reform Bills expanded suffrage, and collective action by workers promoting their interests did not go unnoticed by women. Middle-class women's aspirations, and need, for jobs of their own often reflected a new feminist consciousness that grew out of their experience as single women and widows, frustrated in their efforts to avoid dependence on men. The diary of a self-supported middle-class woman who found her independence, her income, and her very access to her daughter denied when she separated from her husband echoes other feminists in declaring that respectable jobs, including professions, should be available to "honest independent women."[32]

Starting with Lady Caroline Norton's efforts to gain custody of her children, the first organized English feminist movement focused on married women's property rights (including control of their own earnings and child custody in divorce). Barbara Leigh Smith, one of its activists, published a book on *Women and Work* in 1857, and middle-class women—partly through their own efforts, partly through the creation of new jobs or transformation of old ones—slowly gained access to higher education, to such professionalizing occupations as nursing, social work, and teaching, and to a broad range of service occupations such as office and retail clerking. These were designated women's jobs, for the workforce as a whole remained highly segregated, with all women's jobs more poorly paid than men's with similar qualifications. The growth of service occupations expanded women's capability to support themselves and contribute to their families.[33]

Woman suffrage emerged as an issue with John Stuart Mill's amendment to the Second Reform Bill changing the word "man" to "person." It was defeated. By 1900, when a group of Lancashire women textile workers petitioned Parliament in support of suffrage, middle-class suffragettes were actively promoting working-class women's participation in the movement. They found it among textile workers, who were likely to work for wages over long periods (often throughout their lifetimes) and were active in unions. In their persons, the effects of industrialization on women's rights was much more direct than Pinchbeck realized. After an intensive, broadly based campaign for political rights (suspended in the war years) women over thirty were granted the suffrage in 1918, the vote at twenty-one (like men) in 1928.[34]

In the same period, middle-class women mounted a social movement that forced the repeal in 1886 of the Contagious Diseases Acts, laws that imposed medical examinations and possible arbitrary incarceration on women accused of prostitution in cities with an important military presence. The crusaders objected to the acts as immoral and unconstitutional, for they applied a double standard. Some three thousand women ran for and held local public office from the last decades of the century to World War I. Others founded voluntary associations that set up maternal and child welfare programs and agitated for increased government responsibility in the field. Such influential reformers as Beatrice Webb and Helen Bosanquet were members of the Poor Law Commission of 1909. Women were important actors, along with men, in initiating local welfare policies and contributing to the formulation of national welfare legislation. The welfare programs passed by the Liberal government before World War I included old-age pensions, unemployment insurance, and rudimentary health insurance, all of which were contributory, thus involving wage earners in covered industries. Because many women's jobs were not covered, and because few women spent enough years in the labor force to be covered, they were beneficiaries largely through their husbands' earnings.[35]

The British government sought to reduce women's and children's vulnerability by restricting their access to jobs during the time of rapid industrialization. (Would-be reformers sometimes misidentified the problem, and the "protective" laws they sponsored prevented women and children from earning needed wages while leaving exploitative conditions untouched.) This was the period in which middle-class opinion leaders elaborated an ideology of domesticity that became a general goal—for themselves and for workers and their families. Paternalistic employers and women charity visitors pressed working-class women in particular to conform to these new standards. Neither government nor employers' policies were designed to make it easier for married women to work, whether they had to out of necessity or wished to. (Working mothers had to make private arrangements for child care, buy prepared food, and skimp on housework and cleanliness unless their female kin could help them.) Women workers found it hard to take advantage of support programs for mothers and children (at first private, later incorporated into public welfare) because of demanding rules and impractical office hours in such programs; some also objected to intervention in family affairs. Government programs, then, were not always a positive force in improving women's work and home situations; they forbade women to earn wages under conditions perceived as inappropriate or exploitative, but failed to address real needs.[36]

In sum, over the long run the average standard of living rose substantially in Britain for both women and men. Early immiseration of populations whose way of life was undermined by industrialization, and those who endured the unhealthy housing and working conditions and the cycles of boom and bust of the first factory industries, was attenuated by the middle of the nineteenth century. Mortality rates declined, but suggestions of gender inequality in availability of food and health care persisted in the higher death rates of girls and women and in household budget studies (which continued to show female self-denial). Compulsory primary schooling was available free to boys and girls by the end of the nineteenth century, preparing both for better jobs, and educated women were able to get jobs that challenged their capabilities. Both sexes benefited from the fertility decline, but women doubtless experienced greater gains here, and improved capabilities vis-à-vis men. But the division of labor in the household probably became more rigid in middle- and working-class households in which women did not participate formally in the labor force. Wives whose wage work was vital to family wage pooling, such as those in cotton textiles or pottery making, may have gained (or did not lose) leverage in bargaining with their husbands. These same women suffered double burdens because they had major (or full) responsibility for maintaining the household.

In the workplace, women's occupations were restricted and segregated; crowding in few occupations contributed to lower female wages whether an individual worker was supporting herself, and possibly dependents, or whether she was contributing to a family wage. It became rare for men and women to hold identical jobs, but even when they did (cotton weaving) or when women had jobs with qualifications similar to men's (china painters on the potbanks), women's earnings were lower, and they were highly unlikely to have access to supervisory positions or promotion ladders. (Conditions favorable to women in these industries did, however, bring some women into unions and social movements.) Sex segregation was the rule not only in industrial jobs but in most service and many professional jobs as well. Women professionals were often able to support themselves; these women were less likely to marry, either by choice or by circumstance.

The rigidification of job segregation with the increasing scale of production in industrialization—with "housewife" the most segregated job of all—meant continuing gender inequality in both labor market and family. The specifics of these inequalities were determined quite locally. There were few jobs that women never did anywhere, but there were segregated jobs and occupations everywhere. What was skilled, what was heavy work, what was appropriate for men and women—these were a local matter, sometimes bargained between male workers and employers, sometimes decided wholly on employers' prerogatives. Women and children formed a flexible workforce; they entered labor markets in the interstices, serving as helpers to men, holding jobs that did not require long training or had little authority or that men did not want.[37] The family–wage-work nexus, despite an Industrial Revolution, was one in which inequality was inextricably intertwined.

French and German Comparisons

France and Germany began industrialization with economies and political systems that were quite different from the British; hence industrialization in each of these countries followed distinctive paths. The outcomes shared some characteristics with Britain, but differed in important ways as well.

The French kings' drive for centralization and consolidation in the early modern period failed to impose uniform laws or governing institutions (or an adequate fiscal system) in the process of creating a unified territory. Local law and varying forms of local governance with differently negotiated relationships to the monarchy lingered until the French Revolution of 1789–95.

France's eighteenth-century agricultural economy was organized through noble and ecclesiastical landowners, most of whom left the cultivation of their lands (and often decisions about technique and crop) to peasant households that paid customary rent and labor obligations in return. Peasants' holdings became increasingly insecure, while the customary dues and rents they owed their landlords and their taxes (from most of which the higher orders were exempt) rose in the course of the eighteenth century. French agriculture was not highly productive. Although peasants were usually thoroughly involved in markets (at minimum, in order to raise the cash to pay their rent and taxes), they often had to seek means outside agriculture to piece together a living. Protoindustrial entrepreneurs, as in Britain fleeing urban guilds and high costs, offered poverty-stricken households a way to earn wages. Sending household members to cities or wealthy provincial houses as servants was a common peasant survival strategy as well. Although there was specialization in agriculture directed to urban markets, most households continued to produce their own grain. The proportion of the British and French populations engaged in agriculture was similar in about 1750 (65 and 75 percent respectively); what was different was the organization of agricultural production.[38]

France was less urbanized than England, although Paris, like London, was exceptionally large and economically diverse in comparison to provincial cities. Royal policies to encourage urban industry emphasized luxury consumer products such as tapestry, china, and crystal. Private enterprise, operating within France's restrictive economy, nevertheless had expanded substantially (largely in textile production, where reorganization and increased scale were characteristic). Overall rates of economic growth in the eighteenth century were similar to those in Britain, as was the typical urban economy. The guild system persisted in France, however, despite royal efforts to end it, for the monarchy could not afford to pay off the loans that the guilds had made.[39]

Old regime cities were characterized by a gender division of labor. Girls and women usually worked in food, textile, or clothing production or in domestic service. Servants were not specialists in personal service or housework (except in wealthy households); they often spun, wove, sewed or cooked for their employer's business as well. In Lyon, small-scale production of silk was the chief industry; in Le Puy and several cities of the Nord, domestic lace making occupied many women; and in Normandy and Picardy, some large-scale textile mills grouped hundreds of workers. Women workers were integral to the French economy; in most cities, the female jobs they did were similar to those in Britain, as were the conditions—low wages, long hours, and little opportunity for advancement.[40]

The French Revolution ended many of the economic and political barriers to free internal trade and established principles of constitutional rule with broad-based male citizenship and political rights (women were explicitly excluded from such rights during the most radical period of the revolution). It also led to years of warfare with other European nations, which sought to reverse revolutionary changes. The Napoleonic reforms completed centralization and rationalization of government administration. Overall, both urban and rural manufacturing sectors stagnated from 1789 to 1815, except for the few years of peace under Napoleon.

The peasantry benefited from the sweeping away of elite privilege, including fiscal and labor obligations; some were able to buy land or acquire favorable contracts to farm it. Economic growth resumed after 1815 and the return of peace. A centralized monarchy with limited political participation was restored. France's economy was still primarily agricultural with pockets of protoindustry or small-scale manufacturing and some relatively large-scale manufacturing—of cotton textiles in Normandy, Alsace, and the North, and of metal and machines in Lorraine and the south-central reaches of the Loire Valley.[41]

French demography differed from that of England partly because of diverging economic and political conditions, which were accentuated over the revolutionary period. Earlier, as in England, population had been held in check by late marriage and crisis mortality peaks; but during the eighteenth century, the age of marriage increased steadily in France, unlike in England. During and after the revolutionary and Napoleonic periods, fertility control by the couple spread. Both female age at marriage and rates of celibacy declined over the nineteenth century (again unlike England).

Nineteenth-century sociologists believed that the Napoleonic Civil Code lay behind the fertility decline. Although revolutionary legislation included a more liberal family law, the Napoleonic Code both returned to older patriarchal strictures on women's and children's rights in the family and prescribed a uniform partible inheritance system. Landowning or land-controlling peasants, according to some analysts, faced with the possibility of their newly won landholdings being divided among many children, adopted deliberate limitation of births a full fifty years before English fertility rates declined. So too did the bourgeois class, whose property was equally threatened by partible inheritance. Reviewing the literature on French fertility decline, however, the anthropologist Martine Segalen concludes that inheritance law is not a sufficient explanation for fertility decline; ecological, economic, and cultural factors also contributed to it.[42]

Looking briefly at gender relations in nineteenth-century French peasant households, we find Edward Shorter arguing that these households were characterized by extreme gender inequality and female subordination. Wives served husbands and family unquestioningly; in return, they were treated with indifference or contempt. Martine Segalen argues that, to the contrary, the couple's relations were characterized by complementarity, "not absolute authority of one over the other," that grew out of peasant patterns of work and sociability, often done in same-sex groups rather than married couples. A wife's status was enhanced by the economic contribution she made to the household and her ritual and work relationships with water, fire, and thread. Beyond the household economy and community sociability, however, peasant women had few claims to authority or power, while men enjoyed citizenship and voting rights starting in 1848.[43] Given this important caveat, the centrality of women to peasant households and the reciprocal pressure for cooperation in production and reproduction are consistent with Sen's approach, if one adds his notion of conflict as integral to cooperation.

In the 1840s, transportation and communication improved with the building of railroads and the expansion of local roads to integrate formerly isolated areas. Greater interregional—and international—competition among agricultural producers was a consequence that in turn increased specialization and productivity. French urbanization, which also contributed to greater agricultural efficiency, was rapid, proceeding at a rate only slightly lower than that of the British. Nevertheless, the large peasant agricultural sector, and its distinctive gender patterns, continued to be central in French economic and social organization before 1914.[44]

Industrialization was gradual in France, with few sharp discontinuities. Much nineteenth-century economic growth did not involve major transformations of scale or technology. The spinning jenny, which could be used in the household, and the heavier, more expensive mule jenny and water frame were introduced shortly after they were developed in Britain. By 1840, spinning mills in the Nord and Alsace were relatively large scale. Weaving mechanized more slowly (as in Britain), but after the state encouraged railway building, the French cotton industry became competitive on an international scale. The wool and silk industries also reorganized and expanded in the first half of the century, but transformation there was slower than in cotton.

Handloom weaving continued in the north and west, with impoverished hand weavers being paid so little that their products were competitive with machine-woven cloth. In their households a family economy based on the cooperation necessary for survival continued; inherent in that cooperation, however, were also conflicts between parents and children, husbands and wives. Women in the factory textile industry were clustered in less-skilled and poorly paid jobs; they were favored workers in linen spinning and weaving, but in better-paid wool and cotton spinning or weaving, they were more likely to be preparatory workers or helpers. Patterns of segregation varied from one community to another. In the large-scale cotton spinning mills of Roubaix (in the Nord) women circulated at the bottom of the job hierarchy or did preparatory work. In the smaller-scale spinning mills of nearby Amiens, where there were more men's jobs outside textiles, women were likely to hold a wider range of jobs and were excluded only from the top of the job hierarchy.[45]

Heavy industry—mining, metallurgy, and engineering—was the more dynamic sector after midcentury, and it employed primarily men. At the same time, France's early fertility decline and consequently slower population growth produced chronic labor shortages; as a consequence, women more often held jobs (in the machine industry, for example) that would have been male jobs in Britain.

There were distinct, often local, gendered occupational patterns in France, but compared to Britain, these have been little studied. In Limoges, a center of porcelain production comparable to the Potteries of Staffordshire, for example, there are indications of the substitution of less-skilled women plate decorators for highly skilled males who painted designs by hand, and women workers' substantial representation in unions. There is room here for more industry-specific case studies of gender relations.[46]

As in Britain, there were few female jobs in French coal mining areas. Girls and young women did coal sorting at the surface, but married women were much less likely to do wage work, and there was a sharp division of labor within the household. In many mining towns or villages women ran small shops, sewed, or did laundry for their neighbors; or they sold prepared foods, like the "penny capitalists" reported in English towns. Strikes in mining areas were community affairs, with women and children joining demonstrations and attacking nonstrikers.[47]

The French garment industry was characterized by subdivided organization of production and a gendered discourse. Many of the women who sewed "white goods" (underwear, men's shirts, towels, sheets, and so on) lived in the countryside or in smaller cities, as well as in suburbs or poor neighborhoods in Paris; they received the lowest wages of any branch in the industry. Seamstresses who sewed women's outerwear for individual clients might be better paid, especially if they could copy fashionable styles from magazines. In Paris, more elaborate differentiation was the pattern; skilled, well-paid couturières were permanent employees of large outerwear companies and were assisted by less-skilled women with simple specialties. As elsewhere, men dominated the task of cutting garments. The bane of the garment industry was seasonal unemployment, which made the lives of female garment workers very precarious.[48]

In contrast, France's women tobacco workers were in an exceptionally strong labor-market position. They worked in the twenty government manufactories dispersed throughout France. Women made up 80 to 90 percent of the workers in these plants, and they were highly skilled, having undergone an apprenticeship in which they learned all the women's jobs in the industry, including cigar making; these women often worked in teams and developed a group spirit. The jobs were well paid (although women's wages were never as high as men's in the industry) and stable; women tobacco workers responded to these conditions by making lifelong careers in the tobacco monopoly and becoming activists in their unions and major actors in strikes. The government conceded important benefits to women workers: pensions, maternity leave, nursing breaks, and flexible hours when they had infants—even priority for their daughters in applying for jobs in the monopoly.[49]

The large department store revolutionized French (and world) merchandizing in the second half of the nineteenth century; women became clerks as well as customers. The public sector offered women access to clerical and professional jobs (such as postal clerks and teachers) that had career ladders and were awarded on merit. The latter were both rapidly growing occupations in the nineteenth century. A successful experiment utilizing women postal clerks in 1892 led to rapid feminization of clerical services, opposed by the male union and dismayed moralists, but supported by feminists promoting new opportunities for women. Jobs for women teachers opened up when an act requiring compulsory free public schooling was passed in 1882 because schools were sex segregated. Women were perceived to be the most appropriate teachers for girls and younger children. Normal schools were established for training women teachers, including an elite school for teachers destined for female lycées. Children faced examinations at all levels of schooling, and in government service competitive examinations were the key to entry and advancement. When higher-level jobs, such as school inspectors, were opened to women, they were recruited in the same way as men—by examination. This centralized bureaucratic system was favorable to middle-class women's aspirations for *métiers*.[50]

A comparison of the English and French censuses from 1850 to 1960 shows that French women were consistently a higher proportion of the nonagricultural labor force. There was nevertheless considerable sex typing in jobs, depending on sector and local labor markets.[51]

Relatively little research has been reported about husband–wife relations in French working-class households. Husbands' and wives' motives for controlling births may have differed, but the common methods required cooperation by the couple, whether they were peasant or bourgeois. Some working-class groups, such as miners and handloom weavers, and some peasants, were slower to reduce fertility because wage-earning children continued to be critical to families into the twentieth century.[52]

Married women usually had full responsibility for the household budget. Accounts from textile cities report that nonworking wives expected their husbands' full wage packet, out of which they returned spending money. The son of a Parisian working-class couple described his mother's skill in "managing" his father's modest wages. She also moved in and out of the labor force to help make ends meet; his parents were solicitous of their children's needs, but also expected mutual assistance from them. From the Paris suburbs comes a less happy picture: paydays marked by bitter disputes, even blows over how much of a husband's pay was legitimate for his wife to claim. A mother's sense of competence, a contemporary reported, came from her ability to do her job well. A clean, well-fed, and respectably dressed family testified to her managerial skills. In the best situations, the ethic of mutual assistance prevailed; in others, conflict and disagreements were dominant.[53]

In northern France, bourgeois women participated extensively in the management of family businesses during the early development of the textile industry. Many were as a consequence little concerned with the household and child care; they sent their infants to wet nurses and their children to boarding school, instilling in them a strong sense of family loyalty.

Although the bourgeoises of the Nord made critical contributions to the accumulation of physical and human capital, they were excluded by the Napoleonic Civil Code from full participation in business or the public sphere of politics. The increasing scale of industry in the second half of the nineteenth century made it difficult for married women (especially mothers) to operate in both domestic and industrial arenas. Bourgeois women writers defined and prescribed a domestic ideology for women of their class. Through their church-related philanthropic work, careful management of the domestic economy, and practical upbringing of children, these women contributed to the cultural elaboration of their regional middle-class way of life, but much of their visible participation in business disappeared in the Belle Epoque.[54]

The revolutions of 1789 and 1848 saw the emergence of advocates for women's political rights (many of whom had radical or, especially in 1848, socialist connections); they were silenced both times. Moderate feminist groups organized as a new French republic was constructed after 1870. Sensitive to the fragility of national political consensus (and fearing that women's vote might be dictated by Catholic priests), these republican feminists did not demand suffrage and called instead for reform in the civil status of women (through amendment of the Civil Code) and access to education and employment. Those who did call for women's suffrage were rebuffed by secular republicans in power. Women's civil status was somewhat improved by legislation in the years up to 1914 (women were granted control over their own earnings, for example), but the fight for suffrage failed; it was granted only in 1945.

Marital or sexual rights issues, such as eliminating the gender asymmetrical definitions of adultery and earning the right to file paternity suits, were more widely supported, but those calling for divorce or dissemination of information about and devices for birth control split feminists and other women along religious and class lines. Social feminists (here defined as those who promoted women's issues in a broad framework of social reform) cooperated with Catholic charitable organizations that advocated such reforms as the elimination of licensed houses of prostitution, pacifism, and temperance, programs that women moderates could support. The improvement of maternal and infant health was already on the agenda of pronatalists alarmed about "depopulation." Social feminists worked side by side with them for the early state welfare programs: clinics and maternity leaves, as well as public housing and family allowances, seen by the first as encouraging population growth and the second as supporting the poor and vulnerable. Most French social legislation was shaped by concerns about depopulation, but it was supportive of women's childbearing and relatively uncoercive. Nevertheless, the dissemination of birth control information and devices, and abortion, were criminalized. Social programs benefited women as mothers, but they ignored its pronatalist message. There was no comprehensive system of social insurance in France before World War I, as there was in Britain and Germany.[55]

No matter their politics, feminists were nearly all women of means. Women workers often were second-class citizens in the labor movement; tobacco workers and teachers were significant exceptions. Teacher socialist militants were conscious of gender inequality and argued that class-based organizations, such as unions, failed to support women in their everyday family relationships. No feminist and socialist worker alliance emerged because of genuine differences of interest, because most bourgeois feminists were insensitive to the problems of working women, and because most socialist women (despite organizational efforts across class lines) chose to work within unions and socialist groups, rather than with bourgeois feminists.[56]

France's slow industrialization, the continuing importance of its peasant economy, its early fertility decline, chronic labor shortages, and centralized bureaucratic state shaped gender patterns and the timing and content of change in women's capabilities. Thus Frenchwomen were more likely to be independent wage earners or members of household production units than the British, with the disadvantages (low wages, double burden, intense pressures for cooperation, but increased occasions for conflict) and advantages (a wider range of jobs, a material resource—the wage—to bring to household bargaining) that entailed. One result was that the family–productive work nexus seems to have been more benign (despite a similar ideological discourse) in France than in Britain. French middle-class women probably had more opportunities for meaningful jobs, but where their British sisters mounted a successful movement for the vote, the French failed. Differences in religious institutions and political history in the two countries were important factors here. Public policies supported motherhood for pronatalist reasons, but did not interfere with women as workers, so, because of early adoption of family limitation, they were better able to do wage work. French women's legal rights in marriage and suffrage were granted much later than they were in Britain. French economic and political organization mediated the effects of industrialization to produce forms of gender inequality that were different from the British—ones that provided opportunity for women in the economic arena but counted them out of formal politics.

Germany's industrialization was closely linked to its process of political unification, completed in 1871.[57] Indeed, the earlier lack of unity was a major obstacle to German economic development. At the time of the Treaty of Westphalia in 1648, there were about 350 separate political units in Germany; these were combined and simplified only in 1815.

In western Germany, as well as in the east, pressures against peasant landholding were great. Prussian noble landlords (unlike the French) were actively engaged in production of grain for distant markets. Serfdom in Prussia was not a holdover from earlier times but a system tying serfs to the land, instead of subjecting them to lords; a landless proletariat developed in the eighteenth century.

In this period, German urban manufacturing was primarily artisanal, and most states encouraged guild-controlled production of "manufactures," especially luxury goods and weapons; such schemes enjoyed little success. Jean Quataert argues that guilds conflated illegal and "dishonorable" household production and women's domestic work and sought to exclude women from manufacturing for exchange. This history shaped gender ideology and the sex division of labor into the nineteenth century. To the extent that women continued in household-based production for exchange, it was valued less than wage labor outside the household.[58]

Protoindustry nevertheless spread in Germany, producing not the luxury goods that states promoted but cruder textiles and small metalware for popular consumption. These industries contributed to substantial growth in the eighteenth century economy.[59]

French conquest and occupation in the revolutionary and Napoleonic periods united some German states and abolished internal duties. Areas incorporated into the French Empire were encouraged to expand coal and iron production; others stagnated. Napoleon's Continental System, which excluded British products, shielded some areas (the Ruhr Valley, for example) from competition, facilitating growth. In Saxony, large-scale cotton spinning was born. Crushingly defeated by the French in 1806, Prussia instituted economic reforms in order to resist. Serfs were emancipated in 1807 (implemented only after 1810), and limits on individuals' right to choose an occupation were ended in 1808. The Germanic Confederation, established by the peace treaties of 1814 and 1815, was composed of only thirty-nine sovereign states, including Austria. Prussia was awarded Westphalia and parts of the Rhineland, later to become the center of German heavy industry. It took the lead in promoting economic transformation by abolishing internal duties in 1816 and establishing uniform tariffs in all its territories. Railroad building began in 1835 and proceeded so rapidly that by 1875 the German Empire had more railroad mileage than any other continental country. The outcome was a vigorous expansion of markets, and the development of the iron, steel, engineering (railroad locomotives and other machines), textile, and clothing industries.[60]

The German revolutions of 1848 failed to forge a political union with the Austrian lands. In 1866, Prussia provoked a successful war with Austria-Hungary, gaining lands contiguous to its territory. In 1871, after defeating the French, the confederation was transformed into the German Empire, a federation with the king of Prussia as emperor. Universal male suffrage at the level of the imperial Reichstag belied the more limited suffrage in the state legislatures (where fiscal and other important laws were passed) and the authoritarianism of the political system.

During the first two-thirds of the nineteenth century, the rationalization of agricultural landholding proceeded, making possible greater per capita output. Earlier, the sex division of labor on German farms had been relatively flexible, with women often substituting for men, who migrated to find temporary wage work. Childbearing and nurture apparently did not hinder women's labor on the farm. Peasants increased their claims on family labor in agriculture as rural protoindustrial opportunities declined and the cost of hiring day laborers rose. Women's tasks multiplied along with regional specialization in labor-intensive cultivation (potatoes, sugar beets, and other root crops) and stall feeding of animals for butchering. Farm women's increased workload (and probable undernutrition) may have contributed to higher female mortality in adolescence and the early childbearing years, and to infant mortality.[61]

Population increased rapidly in nineteenth-century Germany. Overseas emigration was heavy, especially between the 1840s and 1870, and again in the 1880s. The distances involved in internal migration grew longer as workers moved primarily from the agricultural east to the industrializing west and the older textile areas of Saxony. Could this migration have been an alternative in the east to earlier fertility decline? There has been no conclusive answer to this question, but we do know that female-to-male sex ratios in many of the agricultural sending areas were high, suggesting that women were not only taking over new tasks but were doing routine farm labor as well, because men who had done it in the past were working elsewhere. The earliest signs of German fertility decline began regionally in 1879; the process continued—varying in timing and rapidity from west to east and north to south—until the 1930s.[62]

Coal, iron and steel, and engineering were the leading sectors of German industrialization, responding to the demands of railroad building; the iron industry began its rapid rise in the late 1840s and had caught up with France in terms of annual production by 1870. The Ruhr Valley became a highly concentrated center of heavy industry. Textile mechanization occurred slowly, partly at least because so much of that industry worked with linen (which was both technically more difficult to mechanize and produced for local markets). Germany's comparative advantage in textiles was low wages, and the industry remained smaller scale than the British, selling most of its products in home markets.

Despite the rapidity of these changes, a large part of the German economy and its workers were still involved in small-scale, nonmechanized production. Although domestic production overall declined at the end of the century, it was largely male workers, especially hand weavers, who left to get better jobs elsewhere. Women and child workers became proportionately more important in domestic industry. One possible explanation for this was the new employment code, passed in 1891, that regulated working conditions for firms with over ten workers; children under age fourteen were forbidden to work and required to be in school; women's work hours were limited; and a four-week maternity leave was made compulsory. Women workers in industries that complied with the law were dismissed, but there was widespread noncompliance in industries such as textiles, which depended on women workers. In 1908, an amendment limited adult women to ten hours of work on weekdays, eight hours on Saturday. Household production was wholly unregulated until 1911, when a new law established an inspection system but did not regulate wages. The effort to "protect" women workers by granting them special status in practice limited them to the sector in which exploitation was most likely.[63]

Three manufacturing industries (clothing and cleaning, textiles, and tobacco) employed the largest numbers of women at the turn of the century. Service industries, such as domestic service and inn- and bar-keeping, were the other major employers. In all sectors except textiles, women were concentrated in household or small-scale production. Jobs were segregated by sex and women's wages were one-half to one-third lower than those of unskilled male workers.[64]

Evidence about conditions in industrial homework is abundant. Women who manufactured tobacco products in the household were especially disadvantaged, as were urban clothing workers, domestic servants, and women hand weavers. Nineteenth-century German workers' autobiographies suggest greater misery and family discord compared to the French. Reports of gender conflict increased in the early nineteenth-century records of a Wurttemberg village. A dismal postscript to German women domestic workers' situation is that since women hand spinners, sewers, knitters, and laundresses working in their homes were not covered by the industrial code, they also were not eligible for old-age pensions or health insurance.[65]

Clerical jobs expanded at the end of the nineteenth century, providing new opportunities for women in banking, insurance, shops, and government. These jobs were held primarily by young unmarried women, relatively well educated and possessing some skills (e.g., typing and shorthand), yet poorly paid; clerical work had increased in scale, division of labor, and specialization.[66]

Girls and boys did not have equal access to education in early nineteenth-century Germany despite far-reaching reforms in popular schooling. Literacy—a crude measure of schooling, for there was no one-for-one linkage of literacy and schooling—was lower among women than men in the nineteenth century. Girls were less likely to be schooled in most states. Secondary schools that offered technical training were primarily oriented to transmitting male skills. Advanced public schools intended primarily for middle-class youth were at first closed to females; when they began to admit girls, they were taught domestic skills, not the classic curriculum offered to boys. Women were teachers primarily in the coeducational primary schools. By 1900, eligible children were in schools, male–female differences in attendance had disappeared, and only curricular differences remained.[67]

Women's rights in the family were severely limited up to 1918. Husbands continued to hold full legal guardianship over children, and illegitimate children could not inherit even if their fathers recognized them. Although wives no longer were required to have their husband's permission to do wage work, and they were given control over their own earned income, the property a wife brought into a marriage was fully in the hands of her husband as administrator. Grounds for divorce were strictly limited.

Women's dependency and social inferiority were linked by social commentators and politicians to their biological (thus "natural" and "immutable") characteristics. In the first years of the empire, Prussia and other states had association laws that barred women, apprentices, and schoolboys from membership in political organizations and from attending their meetings. Women found ways to get around these prohibitions, particularly in the Social Democratic party. Only in 1902 did Prussia permit women to attend political meetings if they sat in separate sections—and in 1908 a national law (which superseded state laws) granted women the right of association.

As in France, women's politics, feminist or not, followed the complex fault lines of party politics but, in Germany, the context was an authoritarian state. Following Frederick Engels and August Bebel, the Social Democrats praised the liberating possibilities of participation in social production. Unlike other parties, they hoped to organize and mobilize women as well as men, and unlike middle-class feminists, they supported both female suffrage and protective labor laws to ease the exploitation of women. Based on the assumption that married women belonged in the home, and troubled by the conditions they observed, the Catholic Center party also supported protective laws.

Early middle-class feminist organizations did not make suffrage a primary goal, nor did they think of equality as a natural right. Instead, they conceived of rights as being achieved through women doing their duty, participating in public life (in local institutions), and eventually being granted the rights they had earned. They were more interested in gaining access to jobs and education (not unlike the French) than in abstract rights. By the late 1890s, suffrage became more central, and some feminists argued that women could contribute important feminine qualities to public life, from the courts to the schools to the factories. Modest reforms were proposed, but there was no alliance with socialists because of class differences and incompatible ideologies.

Women socialists developed thriving women's organizations within the bounds of the working class, but they were "reluctant feminists," eschewing women's issues that cut across classes. In 1914 there seemed little prospect of women getting the vote and other political rights in the near future; in 1918, after defeat in war and a revolution, the franchise was granted to women by decree.[68]

In Germany, unlike France, industrialization was rapidly achieved, and its agricultural sector was proletarianized as the peasant household economy was split by male migration to manufacturing or construction jobs in distant regions. German fertility decline followed industrialization with a considerable time lag, as it did in England. Women wage earners were concentrated in nonindustrialized sectors of the economy—household production, domestic service, and agriculture. Women who needed to earn wages were channeled into menial jobs at least partially through legal and ideological barriers. The family–productive work nexus in Germany seems to have been more troubled than the French or the English, with consequences for women's enjoyment of their capabilities.

In the political arena, the presence of a united socialist party with massive working-class support offered some working-class women scope for political participation while preventing them from seeking alliances with feminists, who were either nonpartisan or allied with other parties. Social legislation to relieve workers' insecurity was passed earlier than elsewhere in an unsuccessful effort to coopt workers' support. Redistributive social policies sometimes contributed to gender inequality, as did labor regulation. By 1914, German industrialization had raised the standard of living for German men and women; reform sponsored by feminists and socialists had improved women's legal position in the political arena and in marriage, thus increasing women's capabilities, and fertility decline was under way. New possibilities for clerical employment had opened up, but in 1914 most women's jobs were still clustered in agriculture and manufacturing, especially at the low waged, labor-intensive level. And gender inequality prevailed in the household. Women's capabilities had expanded, but so had men's, and there were few net gains for women.

The United States

European settlers in North America appropriated a relatively sparsely populated but fertile and spacious land from its Native American inhabitants. From the earliest settlement, agricultural development and its accompanying social organization differed regionally. In the North was a combination of independent family farms and greater urbanization; in the South, large-scale plantation and smaller farm cultivation of tobacco with hired or African American slave labor was more typical. In the eighteenth century, the North became more urban and commercial and began to industrialize, while the southern plantation economy spread, switching from tobacco to cotton cultivation. Labor was in short supply everywhere, so wages were better than those in Britain, attracting immigrants seeking a better life; the "coerced migration" of Africans was also substantial, partly because of their high mortality during passage and in the new disease environment.

The American Revolution was a rejection by the British colonists not only of their collective dependent position vis-à-vis Britain but also of the political and social order of European states. In its place was founded a decentralized state, in which authority was concentrated in the central government, but many political institutions and functions were controlled by the states.

The first water-powered mill was opened in 1790 in Rhode Island, but it was the dearth of manufactured imports during the War of 1812 that stimulated American industrialization. As in Britain, the process began in the cotton industry, where factory production first replaced household spinning, then weaving. The Lowell, Massachusetts, textile mills offered jobs in the 1820s and 1830s primarily to adolescent and young adult women from farm families. These workers' earnings were a transitional stage in their lives; they worked to contribute to a brother's education, to save for their own future marriage, or perhaps for some costly personal project, such as further schooling. They were also distinguished by their consciousness of their rights and willingness to strike for them. The textile industry's expansion ended in the depression of the last years of the 1850s.

By the 1840s, and even more in the 1850s, increasing immigration had eliminated labor shortages, and cotton mill owners found immigrant families from Ireland and French Canada both cheaper and more quiescent workers. Later in the nineteenth and in the first decades of the twentieth century, these immigrant men and women and their children would be both constrained and supported by their household and kin relationships. Before the Civil War, rural workers in household production of hand-woven textiles, palm hats, and shoes labored in small towns and the countryside, far from factories.[69] A progression from small-scale to factory production occurred in the boot and shoe industry in and around Lynn, Massachusetts. In the eighteenth century, women had sewed uppers as assistants to skilled male household members; at the end of the century, shoemaking was partially transformed into protoindustry, as girls and women worked longer hours, and more regularly. The industry mechanized and concentrated in the 1850s (over the protest of skilled males losing their monopoly of the trade), and women followed their jobs into factories.[70]

In the antebellum period, only a small proportion of women worked outside their homes, most of them single women, and an even smaller proportion worked in manufacturing—small scale (e.g., bookbinding) or large (e.g., cotton spinning). Domestic service was the most common sector for women's wage work; like the mill workers, servants were increasingly likely to be immigrants from Europe. Free African American women in the North were excluded from work in factories or skilled jobs; they were likely to be laundresses, cooks, or sometimes seamstresses. In the largely plantation-organized agricultural South, slave labor predominated. Rural areas with available water power housed cotton mills, and the various consumer industries—garment making, food preparation, construction, and skilled crafts—were located in cities; garment and food industries were female, and the latter were largely white male domains. Northern urban economies were not so different, except that immigrants took the place of slaves at the bottom of the occupational hierarchy. Male immigrants were also recruited to build canals and then railroads, which improved transportation on the east coast and toward the west. Many Americans continued to seek opportunity in agriculture and moved westward to find land.[71]

The Civil War opened new jobs in white-collar work for women with education or training—as clerks, professional nurses, and teachers. (The expansion of clerical and professional work for women is considered later.) Working-class women, mobilized for war work (sewing uniforms primarily) or filling in for absent male workers in urban industries had a more difficult time because they had little recourse against exploitative conditions. As individual workers, women were in a particularly weak position, for they often desperately needed jobs but had little work experience.

Dissatisfaction continued in the garment industry after the war ended.

Sewing machines had been introduced in the war years, and women worked either in workshops or at home, for extremely low wages. Where seamstresses had formerly learned varied skills, now the jobs were broken into discrete tasks, and the garment was passed from worker to worker, each with her specialty. Despite such disadvantages, Carole Turbin shows, Troy women collar makers were successful in organizing a union, partly at least because they had support from men—some of them kin—in the town's iron molding industry; collar workers also set up a cooperative laundry when they lost their jobs in a lockout.[72]

The post–Civil War period saw rapid growth in large-scale grain milling, meat slaughtering and packing, metal and machine production, and mining. Replacement of skilled male workers by women or less-skilled immigrants continued. In newspaper printing, employers attempted to undermine the apprenticeship system and strong organization of males by training literate women to do the job more cheaply. Male printers saw their masculinity compromised by women's competition, but accepted the linotype machine. With male workers' support, employers defined it as requiring endurance, hence boys and men were operators.[73]

Metal and machine manufacturing workers, mostly male, such as Troy's skilled iron molders, suffered deskilling with technological change and reorganization of the labor process. A view of such changes from the perspective of gender and family shows that, in the period in which Pittsburgh switched from iron to steel making and the mill labor process was subdivided, women's unpaid work in household maintenance and childrearing was essential. The sharp household division of labor in such cities promoted fragile gender relations in families. Women's wage work in Pittsburgh—less common than in cities with a more mixed industrial character—was segregated not only by gender but by race and ethnicity and was poorly paid. The ways in which migration and urban economic change affected ethnic women's work and family lives in less specialized urban settings, such as New York, also involved both cooperation and conflict.[74]

Racial segregation and tensions in southern industry reduced the possibility of workers' coalitions in the early twentieth century, undercutting both class and female solidarity in labor organizing and struggle. In the North Carolina tobacco industry, manufacturers of tobacco products constructed a workforce ingeniously stratified by race and sex as early as the 1880s. White women operated the newly developed cigarette-making machines; white men supervised them and maintained the machines; black men handled the heavy bales of tobacco and the fermentation process; and black women specialized in stemming tobacco leaves. At least temporary cooperation across race and class occurred in the southern textile industry as well. Cross-cutting class, gender, and ethnic divisions affected both middle- and working-class women's activism in Florida. A comparison of male and female labor process and work culture in cigar making as the occupation was mechanized and deskilled illustrates the contrary trends of gendered access to skill and displacement of skilled workers.[75]

Women workers' efforts to organize and strike, as well as their sometimes troubled relations with labor unions, have received a good deal of attention. Conventional historical accounts of the important Lawrence, Massachusetts, textile strike of 1912 that emphasize the role of the International Workers of the World (IWW) have been challenged by gender-centered revision. The garment industry strikes that occurred across the country in the same period have also been reexamined: The International Ladies Garment Worker's Union's (ILGWU) women workers and organizers lost a corset strike in Kalamazoo, Michigan, to intransigent employers despite appeals for support across class lines to middle-class women. The Rochester, New York, Chicago, Cleveland, and most famous of all, New York City garment industry uprisings were also characterized by complex relationships of women workers with male trade union leaders and middle-class women who wished to support but also control their struggle. The Women's Trade Union League was central to many of these efforts.[76]

The debate on the family wage that has engaged British women's historians has an American counterpart. The family wage (a male wage adequate to support a family) was originally a working-class cause that united men and women. Only in the twentieth century did it become an exclusively male ideal supported as well by some employers and middle-class reformers.[77]

The efforts of women industrial workers to organize in their interests and strike, even if successful, changed the relationship of their wages to men's only to the extent that occupational segregation declined (men workers dominated in better-paying jobs and better-paying industries, and they were more often organized in unions that could win better conditions). Claudia Goldin's painstakingly assembled wage-ratio series show a modest rise in the manufacturing earnings ratio in women's favor from 1850 to about 1885 when it reached .56; since then, despite cyclical fluctuation, it has "not materially budged." Around 1881 to 1907, when moral concerns about female employment peaked, women were likely to work more continuously than contemporaries believed, but their total job experience was relatively brief, for they exited the workforce promptly upon marriage, and the vast majority never returned. Because of employers' perceptions, women were limited to dead-end jobs and seldom received training; males had much longer total work experience, longer duration in current occupation and with current employer. Goldin concludes that only 20 percent of the wage differences can be laid to strictly defined "wage discrimination."

The gender wage ratio among *all workers* continued to narrow until the 1930s. This improvement primarily reflected the changing sectoral distribution of women's occupations, in particular the rise of clerical jobs, which were more desireable: cleaner, more respectable, and better paid. They also were at first less segregated, and wages at first hire were similar for the two sexes. A 1940 survey with comparable information on characteristics of individual male and female clerical workers again reveals similar initial wages, but, by this time, an extremely segregated workforce, with women limited to occupations with little possibility for advancement. (Men too were limited to specific occupations, but these were on career ladders.) For Goldin, this reflects "statistical discrimination" in personnel policies that treated women as a group having limited commitment and more likely to leave the labor force than men. Deliberate and conscious policies of sex segregation had become the norm sometime early in the twentieth century.[78]

Goldin's analysis is the most comprehensive done so far, but questions linger in her mind about the extent to which women in manufacturing arrived at the workplace with characteristics already shaped by discrimination and social expectations. There are also suggestions that employers simply sought women for low-waged jobs and men for responsible and better-paid ones. She notes an unexplained "bonus" paid only to married men and speculates whether employers had a notion of a "fair" wage for men. Only in her last chapter does she bring up the issue of women's disproportionate responsibility for children and the household.

The earliest movement of women workers from manufacturing to clerical occupations occurred in the Civil War temporary mobilization of women into government service, as Cindy Aron shows. It accelerated with the expansion of office work connected with large-scale industry, and of banking and insurance at the end of the century. The size of commercial enterprises selling consumer products also increased remarkably. Typewriters, telephones, mechanical bookkeeping machines, and cash registers became women's machines after 1890. Native-born, white, young women with a modicum of education poured into the ranks of clerical workers. In both merchandising and office work there was a good deal of subdivision of tasks and specialization in the labor process.[79]

American middle-class women resemble the British most closely in their involvement with class formation primarily through the domestic sphere (and its social extension in philanthropy and improvement of society) and in the elaboration of an ideology of domesticity, as Mary Ryan shows in her study of Oneida County, New York, from 1780 to 1865. Earlier patriarchal gender relations in the family disappeared in a burst of evangelical revivalism starting in 1814, which lasted until 1838. Women were the first converts to evangelicalism and sponsored the early revivals, changing the name of their Female Charitable Society to the Oneida Female Missionary Society. By the mid-1820s, men had assumed a more active role in revivalism and women retreated to the "home," where they raised their children and smoothed the way for male success in the business world. Women continued to be active in churches and in charitable and mutual support groups (the Maternal Association, for example). American fertility decline began early in the nineteenth century among white women, and (as measured by live births per 1,000 white women aged 15–44) had declined by 30 percent in 1850 and another 33 percent by 1900.

Within-class material conditions and ideological dispositions lie behind systematic variation in women's activity in urban benevolent, reform, and radical associations in the same period. A study of Tampa, Florida, at the turn of the twentieth century finds an "astonishing array of voluntary associations" of middle-class women concerned with the social changes associated with industrialization.[80]

The links between these associations and the women's suffrage movement are Suzanne Lebsock's focus in a synthetic essay that draws on recent monographic studies to map women's voluntarism in the public sphere. By 1890, women had a hundred-year record of fighting—most often in single-sex groups—for temperance, abolition of slavery, prison reform, education, better jobs and higher wages, women's rights in marriage, and suffrage. The Women's Christian Temperance Union (WCTU) was the paradigmatic case, mobilizing women under the banner of protecting the home. The Young Women's Christian Association (YWCA) offered social services to urban single women; women's clubs sought to beautify their towns and build hospitals; settlement houses hoped to help the destitute, support women and children, clean up urban politics, and promote social harmony; the birth control movement took up issues not ordinarily discussed and dispensed advice and devices; and the Women's Trade Union League sought to improve women's working conditions. Progressive women were influential in the passage and judicial acceptance of protective legislation that restricted the industries and conditions in which women could work. Later, still others chose to work with men in political parties—Republican, Democratic, Populist, Socialist—or in nonpartisan local reform politics to create welfare programs or fight corrupt politicians. African American middle-class women also participated in single-sex clubs and the Republican party, seeking to improve the social and political position of their people. Women's broad involvement with issues in the public arena contributed to their belief that suffrage was a prerequisite for achievement of their ambitious agenda. Their associational activity provided experiences that stood them in good stead in the suffrage campaign. In 1920, the Nineteenth Amendment granted women the right to vote.[81]

The United States differed from European countries in its seemingly limitless resources, its decentralized and participatory political system, and its opposition to federal government action in economic and social matters (modified only partially in the Progressive era). Temporal change in the ratio of women's to men's wages suggests that industrialization substantially improved that ratio through women's transfer first from agriculture to manufacturing and later from manufacturing to clerical jobs. In both sectors, however, there was an apparent "glass ceiling," as contemporary analysts have come to call it, by which employer policies, hostile male workers' opposition, and majority women's acceptance of social expectations ended further improvement.

By 1914, industrialization had improved the standard of living of the population as a whole, and fertility decline was achieved. Schooling, although it varied in quality and quantity from state to state, had achieved a minimum standard for white boys and girls; both were more likely to have access to secondary school than were Europeans. Working- and middle-class women were ably defending their perceived interests as well as promoting their vision of social good, activities facilitated by government decentralization. American women's high level of activism distinguishes them from continental Europeans and the British as well; many of the capabilities women gained in the period were at least partly the result of women's own efforts, although their activism was broader than the simple promotion of gender interests. They had clearly achieved high levels of capability. Nevertheless, problems remained: the sex division of labor in the household, gender segregation in the workplace, the barrier to further progress toward wage equality, and the unachieved agenda for women in electoral politics.

Japan

Economic and demographic changes in the last century of the preindustrial Tokugawa period (1602–1867) prepared the way for the more far-reaching transformation that began in the 1870s, after the Meiji Restoration of 1868.

The greater part of the Japanese population in the Tokugawa period was engaged in agriculture (estimates run from around 76 to 83 percent). Of the agrarian population, about 75 percent were peasant proprietors, who owed high land dues to their lord; the rest were tenants, who paid rent. The common unit of production was the household, hence holdings were small. Urban population growth promoted the development of markets, increasing productivity, migration (in theory, illegal), and rural handicraft production. Farm size declined with improved methods of cultivation stressing labor intensity, as larger holdings were subdivided and rented to tenants whose families were their labor force. Peasant living standards were very low, but agriculture became highly productive.

Manufacturing was not as dynamic as agriculture; it was divided between urban crafts organized in guilds producing fine textiles, clothing, decorative objects, food, or buildings and rural industry organized on a household basis by urban putters-out to spin and weave cruder fabrics. Larger-scale production of reeled and spun silk, iron, and sake had begun. Commerce was lively, and a road system was well advanced, partly because local lords (who lived in fortified castle cities with military retainers, servants, artisans, and merchants) were expected to spend long periods each year in the capital, Edo (now Tokyo). The castle cities were themselves important markets; they had developed fiscal and administrative specialization that prepared samurai landlord elites for leadership in later government-promoted economic development.[82]

Studies of the demographic and family changes that accompanied the gradual economic change of the Tokugawa period provide insight into the comparative capabilities of men and women in preindustrial Japan. The emergence of couple-headed households as the unit of agricultural production utilizing new technologies first spurred rapid population growth, followed by a static period, as Japanese peasant couples apparently began deliberately limiting fertility early in the nineteenth century.

How were households formed, and how did they pass on headship to the next generation? Stem households were typical; their rules permitted several generations of married couples in one household, but no more than one from any generation; the inheriting child was selected by the parents, but there was flexibility about which one was chosen. If there were no children, a child could be adopted as heir; when there were no male children, a male might be adopted to marry the inheriting daughter; noninheriting children were sometimes established in branch households.

Temporary (in intent, at least) out-migration to jobs in nearby agriculture or household handicraft industries was common and increased in the nineteenth century for both men and women—a kind of life-cycle service. Many women migrants ended their travels with marriage, at a significantly older average age than women who stayed in their parents' household. Work in handicraft production in one village was similarly connected to women's marriage age advancing by almost two years, as well as to a decrease in the differentially high female infant and child mortality rates. Young women benefited from contributing to their natal household's well-being; a higher age at marriage meant fewer years at risk of childbearing. Although divorce was quite common, compared to the mid-twentieth century, its consequences for women were less serious than its male-initiated arbitrary manner would suggest. This was true because divorce usually occurred early in marriage, remarriage was quite likely, and although the children were usually taken from their mother, they were likely to be valued and well cared for in their father's household.[83]

In preindustrial Japan, then, women's economic productive capabilities were valued relatively higher when wage-earning opportunities existed for them. Both men and women in country or city expected to marry, and in agriculture especially, a *couple* was indispensable for a viable household production unit. Anthropologists studying a remote farming village in the 1930s concluded that the peasant household structure and division of labor led to full interdependence of the couple.[84]

In 1867, disaffected samurai overthrew the shogun and restored the Emperor Meiji; their goal was to resist Western encroachment through rapid indigenous industrialization. Relatively efficient production of military weapons had begun in the Tokugawa period, but after the restoration the sector was quickly industrialized with state support. Large-scale textile industrialization was achieved by buying technology and know-how from Europe, again with initial government support. Rapid growth in agricultural land and labor productivity that met increased food demand (based on increasing per capita income) underwrote industrialization. Key improvements included better irrigation and drainage, better strains of food crops, and increased use of fertilizer. The agricultural productive unit continued to be the small farm household paying high taxes or, if tenants, high rents in kind, and expelling "surplus" young people (often females whose labor was less needed in cultivation) in a sometimes coerced migration to earn wages in urban industry.[85]

Japanese industrialization was "self-financed" by agriculture; the largest source of government income before World War I was the Meiji Land Tax of 1873. Political pressure for economic change, in which export-oriented textile production was critically important, not consumer demand, promoted Japanese development.

Henry Rosovsky believed that the textile labor force was recruited and retained through paternalistic policies that promoted worker loyalty. Although he admitted that the ideal was necessarily far removed from actuality, historians who have looked in more detail at women's jobs and working conditions have challenged this conclusion. The economic historian Gary Saxonhouse first called attention to the problems textile employers had in keeping their young female workers, who ran away regularly; high turnover continued into the 1930s, even after workers' situation improved. His analysis shows that entering cotton spinners had *lower* wages than female agricultural workers; hence they themselves were bearing the cost of training. If they left before their contract was up, however, they could easily find work elsewhere, as skills were similar among mills. Employers did not succeed in solving the problem of worker turnover until after World War II.[86]

The large-scale Osaka Cotton-Spinning Mill (opened in 1883) set the model for two practices that became central to Japanese cotton production: fine grading of job categories in which female's piecework wages were never higher than 58 percent of male and usually less; and shift work, with two twelve-hour shifts daily. By the mid-1890s, the supply of female workers within commuting distance from large mills had been tapped, and mill owners began to build dormitories to house country girls who lived farther away.

Recruiters went to the countryside with tempting offers of good wages, pleasant working conditions, and tasty food; impoverished families willingly signed contracts committing their daughters to long terms in the mills in return for advance cash loans. Daughters dutifully reported for work, only to discover filthy, locked dormitories; long workdays (and night shifts); brutal supervisors; and disciplinary fines withheld from their wages so that neither parents or daughters got the promised wages. Men were more often recruited locally and lived at home; they usually became mule spinners or machine menders and were paid higher salaries; women and girls were ring spinners, piecers, and assistants.[87]

By the 1920s, young women were more likely to have completed at least primary schooling, and they often chose to do factory work not only to help their parents but also to achieve their own goals. Fewer went back to rural areas to marry and raise families. Although conditions were still bad, they had improved at least partly because of strikes in major mills; after 1929, middle-class feminists and reformers persuaded the government to implement laws prohibiting child labor and women's late-night work, and the hours in each shift were cut. As women became more likely to stay with a firm longer, they were promoted to better positions.[88]

Silk reeling had been organized in Tokugawa times in both centralized filatures and merchant-organized putting out, using an improved type of reel. At the end of the period, some entrepreneurs separated the process of reeling from the cultivation of silkworms and set up more efficient mills, using French equipment and technicians; samurai landlords' daughters taught the new techniques to other women. As more labor was needed, poorer girls were recruited and housed in dormitories; they became "a class of temporary indentured servants or debtors," according to Gail Bernstein. Limited mechanization in silk reeling contributed to constant pressure on the women to work faster yet produce high-quality yarn. Nevertheless, it is not clear that the conditions of industrial spinners and reelers were worse than those of impoverished rural families or in prostitution (which together employed many more women workers than cotton spinning and silk reeling). The proportion of women workers in Japanese manufacturing continued to be higher than in the West. This reflected the importance of textile production and the continuing availability of rural females for employment in that industry.[89]

Before turning to the state's definition of women's role in the Meiji period and middle-class women's response, a brief look at women in the

Tokugawa merchant class is in order. Local custom in Osaka permitted women to act temporarily as household heads and indeed a certain number of them seized opportunities to run family businesses on this basis or in cooperative but subordinate relationships with male heads (fathers, husbands, or sons). Although only males were permitted to do the actual brewing of sake, several women ran very sucessful family sake businesses. Tatsu'uma Kiyo (1809–1900) was the power behind a sake brewery she managed with the help of an able male brewmaster. Her shrewd business sense was applied as well to family affairs: The marriages of her six children were veritable business alliances.[90]

The chief object of Meiji policymakers was to mobilize all resources, including people, in the pursuit of their twin goals: industrialization and national power. Hereditary restrictions on occupation and residence were quickly abolished so that an industrial workforce could be recruited. The Meiji Constitution of 1889 granted suffrage to males (based on property tax paid) in elections to the lower house of Parliament. Policies about women and the family took shape more slowly. In 1873, the government mandated compulsory public education for both boys and girls; in the same decade, elite women were permitted to play limited public roles similar to those in the West.

The early feminists, associated with liberal reformers, sought to win equal opportunity in education and work, legal rights in marriage, divorce, property holding, and the vote. In 1890, however, a Law on Associations and Meetings forbade women to attend public meetings (amended only in 1922), or join political parties (in force until 1945). Apparently, women's family and home duties, not their incapacity, were the justification for their exclusion. The Meiji Civil Code of 1898 "samurized" family relations, imposing samurai principles on the population at large: Husbands and fathers were granted absolute power as household heads; wives were considered legally without competence. An 1899 law opened secondary schools to girls; they were to be taught to be "good wives and wise mothers." During the Japanese wars around the turn of the century, women were mobilized in support of the war effort to serve as nurses and distribute assistance to widows and orphans. The feminine virtues that the state wished to see cultivated were modesty, courage, frugality, literacy, hard work, and productivity; neither motherhood nor domesticity was central in the period.[91]

As in Western countries, the service sector, which began to expand especially in the second decade of the twentieth century, opened up new jobs for women. Longer schooling qualified girls for jobs as teachers, social workers, nurses, telephone operators, government workers (here postal and railroad clerks were important), and other clerical work. Middle-class women sought these jobs out of need, because of heightened consciousness, or because they were increasingly available. Although some married women were in the labor force, most female workers were single; their wages were substantially lower than men's (sometimes as low as one-third of male wages for comparable skills).[92]

In the 1930s, as Japan again went to war with its neighbors, the contradiction between women's wage work and their demanding reproductive responsibilities became more acute. The slogans "good wife, wise mother," which exalted women's role in preserving the Japanese family system, and "rich country, strong army," which pushed women's contribution to industrialization, proved to be irreconcilable. Women were both urged to bear more children and mobilized into patriotic associations; a mother–child protection law designed to help single mothers raise their young children was passed in 1937. Motherhood was conceptualized in new ways. Some Japanese feminists collaborated with these war policies as a step toward gender equality because they permitted women a *public* role. In the end, the campaign for higher fertility was contradicted by the drive to hire women for what were formerly men's jobs. Although women were only drafted for war work in 1944, the experiences of the 1930s and the war years prepared the way for postwar changes.

In 1948, the patriarchal household family system (*ie*) was legally replaced by a nuclear family system in which husbands and wives had equal standing. Although initially insignificant, married women's wage work has increased in the postwar period, but men's and women's relationship to jobs and careers remains very different. Male labor unions emphasize firm-specific workplace conditions and stability, rather than collective bargaining about wages; women workers are perceived as needing protection. A structural dualism has emerged with a male elite enjoying lifetime employment and "needing" full-time wives to support the work commitment such a system required. The female–male wage ratio, 52, is the lowest among industrialized countries. Japanese women still usually leave their jobs when they marry and thereafter work only part time. State policy continues to be shaped by the principle that women's only proper role is familial; this ideology is accepted by the majority of men and women alike, and by such institutions as firms and labor unions. The Equal Employment Opportunity Law of 1986 has done little to change business policies that implicitly assume such a gender division of labor in the household and workplace.[93]

The distinctive characteristics of Japanese industrialization—the Meiji government's central role in promoting economic development and its translation into law of earlier ideals of the patriarchal household that had until then been only imperfectly reflected in ordinary people's lives—seem to have effectively limited any trend toward gender equality. Women were important contributors to the process of industrialization, as members of agricultural households on which the tax burden of the process fell, and as low-waged workers in its leading sector, cotton textiles. Although women shared the rising standard of living with men of their class, as well as reduced fertility, longer schooling, expanded participation in politics, and marriage and family law that theoretically is more equitable, the inflexibility of the division of labor in the household and lack of opportunity in the workplace continue to prevent full enjoyment of their capabilities.

China

Long before the British Industrial Revolution, Western countries had impinged on the rest of the world through trade, conquest, and colonization; industrialization increased the wealth and strength of the West and produced greater disparities between developed and less-developed regions.[94]

Although China as a whole was never a colony (as were many non-Western countries), in the nineteenth and twentieth centuries its resources and labor were tapped by foreign capitalists who enjoyed economic, political, and legal privileges not very different from those in colonies. At the same time, China maintained its language and culture and continued to produce thinkers and movements that were quite distinctive, shaped by the history and tradition, large size, and ethnic and ecological diversity of the country.[95] Nineteenth-century Chinese governments and private enterprise, like those of Japan, sought to promote industrialization, but Chinese development gathered force only after World War I, especially in the late 1920s and early 1930s, and again after World War II, under socialist auspices. Both China's Nationalist and Communist revolutionary policies were more consciously gender egalitarian in principle that those in earlier industrializing national states, Western or Japanese. China is not typical of late industrializing non-Western states, but it offers an opportunity to look at questions about the effect of factors present in many parts of the contemporary developing world on gender inequality up to the present.

From 1644 to 1911, the Qing dynasty, Manchu conquerors from the north, ruled China. The first century and a half of their rule saw systemization of the bureaucracy, renovation and extension of the canal system providing better transportation of goods and people, the development of new crops and flourishing crafts, increased monetization of the economy, and efficient tax collection. It also made possible population expansion.

John King Fairbank attributes the strongly patriarchal organization of families (with inheritance shared among male offspring, arranged marriages, patrilocal residence of married sons, and extreme subordination—exemplified by foot binding, a cruel custom that in northern China was common even among peasants—of women as daughters and daughters-in-law) to China's high population density, in addition to the more conventional explanation, the Confucian worldview. He emphasizes as well the "remarkable integration of state, society, and culture" and the highly bureaucratic state. By the end of the eighteenth century, population pressure, together with political corruption and social divisions (between men and women, old and young, landlords and tenants), had produced a highly volatile political situation.[96]

The imperial government, weakened by antirent and antitax rebellions, was unable to prevent opportunistic British export of opium from India to China. A British punitive expedition in 1839 against Canton, then against other coastal cities, opened the Opium Wars. The 1842 peace treaty imposed a huge fiscal indemnity on China, guaranteed British extraterritoriality (legal and political rights under English law in designated places in China) and granted missionaries the right to move freely around the country. A civil war—the Taiping Rebellion—gathered force in the 1850s, to be repressed only with Western assistance in 1864. (The Taipings were a millenarian sect professing a heterodox monotheistic religion incorporating elements of fundamentalist Protestantism.)

As in Japan at about the same time, elements within the government promoted a "self-strengthening" industrialization to produce arms and ships for military preparedness. It had few results. "Compradore capital" accumulation was more successful. Chinese merchants worked first with foreign firms, later on their own account, to develop silk filatures, steamship lines, coal mines, and cotton spinning and weaving companies (not subsidized but often supervised by government agencies) in the 1870s to 1890s.[97]

Foreign interventions and wars continued, however. As China faced the threat of partition in 1898, a liberal reform group persuaded the emperor to begin institutional and economic reforms. The effort lasted only a hundred days, ended by a seizure of power by the conservative traditionalist dowager empress. Despite the failure to reform the state and economy, new ideas began to circulate as greater freedom of speech, press, and association permitted debate among intellectuals and students. Again rebellion and foreign intervention interrupted the process, this time the 1900 antiforeign Boxer uprising in Shandong. The United States renewed its call for an "open door" to foreign commerce, and the Germans, British, Russians, and Japanese agreed to end territorial seizures in China. The settlement humiliated the Qing dynasty and revealed its powerlessness.

Discussion and reform groups, among them Sun Yat-sen's Revive China Society, which preached an anti-Qing nationalist, vaguely social democratic program, proliferated. New government reforms included the elimination of the daunting classical civil service examinations, the establishment of practical schools, and greater possibilities for Chinese to study abroad in Japan and later in Europe and the United States. A mutiny in 1911 (supported by the military and secret societies) against the recently ascended boy emperor led to the declaration of a republic. Sun Yat-sen was forced out of the presidency, and a promonarchy dictatorship was established instead (most Nationalists opposed this regime). During World War I, China seized the German and Austrian concessions, and its native industry thrived as Western imports disappeared from domestic markets.

When the Versailles Treaty was publicized, intellectuals and students vigorously objected to its stipulation that Japan would receive German rights and territorial concessions in Shandong Province. Protest on May 4, 1919, forced the government to refuse to sign the treaty and launched a revolutionary movement in which the Nationalist party (the Kuomintang [KMT]) and—after 1921 when it was founded in Shanghai—the Chinese Communist party (CCP) were uneasily allied. (In response to May 4, the young Mao Zedong organized a progressive society in Hunan.) The Soviet Russian-led Communist International advised the CCP to collaborate with the KMT but keep its own identity for later opposition and communist revolution.

Despite the pious declarations of an eight-power international conference in Washington in 1921–22, respecting Chinese sovereignty and agreeing to work for stability in the country, a period of regional warlordism and intergroup struggles ensued. Sun Yat-sen (then head of an independent KMT-governed region whose military aide in his last years was young Chiang Kai-shek) died in 1925. In 1927 the Communists were expelled from the KMT, and civil war became general. In 1928, the Nationalists under Chiang declared a nominally unified nationalist republic, which succeeded over the next eight years or so in promoting economic development and keeping order in many areas. It failed, however, to prevent the Japanese seizure of Manchuria in 1931, followed by further incursions into Chinese territory. In this period, through their experience in controling a territory in the southeast (the Jiangxi Soviet), the Communists developed strategies for mobilizing peasant military and economic support. The Communists were nevertheless forced to retreat to northern China (Shensi Province) in 1934 on the Long March, during which they suffered enormous losses.

In 1936, dissident warlord KMT troops captured Chiang; their Soviet advisers persuaded the Communists to seek his freedom and unite with the KMT to fight the Japanese. The cooperative effort failed. The Nationalists were weakened by their long fight against Japan and by corruption in their army, while the Communists enjoyed strong grass-roots support. Conflict between the two parties resumed. As World War II ended, the Communists held extensive rural bases in northern and central China, and the KMT nominally controlled the south. Starting in 1945 the Communist People's Liberation Army (PLA) conquered mainland China, and on October 1, 1949, declared the People's Republic of China (PRC).[98]

Mao Zedong was the PRC's undisputed leader in 1949, working with an experienced and tested team. Fairbank divides the period from 1949 to the present into economic and political consolidation to 1958, two great popular mobilizations supported by nongovernmental groups outside the party leadership—the Great Leap Forward (GLF, 1958–60) and the Great Proletarian Cultural Revolution (GPCR, 1966–69)—with the intervening and succeeding periods more focused on economic development.

In the postrevolutionary period, rural land redistribution virtually eliminated the landlord class, and in urban areas Communist cadres achieved first consolidation and then "socialist transformation" (1955–57). The 100 Flowers Campaign in 1956–57 encouraged criticism of the party, but those who took advantage of the more open discussion soon found themselves labeled rightists. The GLF program (starting in 1958) sought to increase productivity through increased socialist organization of the rural economy, that is, rural people's communes and producers' cooperatives. Agricultural production increased in the first year of the GLF, but in 1959–60 crop failure and a devastating famine that killed millions haunted the program. The attempt to decentralize industrial production also failed. Under fire, Mao began a rectification campaign to educate the peasants through struggle sessions with intellectuals and bureaucrats; it failed to reduce the importance of elites. He then went outside the party for help in rectifying their errors.

In the GPCR, Red Guards attacked cultural figures and party officials in what Mao conceived as a revitalization of revolutionary values. The campaign included ultraleftist bullying that disrupted production and social relations; by mid-1968, Mao was forced to demobilize the Red Guards and call on the army to restore order. Antinatalist fertility-control policies were begun in urban areas in the period; they were extended to the whole country in 1970. From then until Mao's death in 1976, the military backed attempts by his old companions in arms, like Zhou Enlai, to rebuild the party and government. Those of Mao's associates who tried to prolong the Cultural Revolution were attacked after his death as the Gang of Four.

The slogan of the Four Modernizations has since become the watchword; rural to urban migration was closed off; rural collectivization was scaled back and replaced by the "household responsibility system," which provides incentives for agrarian families to produce; China was opened to foreign trade, technology, and investment; industrial policy was changed from self-sufficiency based on heavy industry to export-oriented light industry; banking has been decentralized; and the one-child family has been proclaimed as the norm in an effort to level off population growth.[99]

How does gender, women's work, and the sex division of labor fit into this panoramic sweep of rebellion, war, reaction, idealistic goals, and the mixed record of Communist revolution?

The first modern histories of Chinese women focused on the extremes of inequality to which they were subjected in traditional China—the material miseries of female peasants and workers and the social and psychological denial of identity to upper-class women; women heroes of rebellion and revolution; and the oppositional ideas of cultural figures, reformers and revolutionaries, whether men or women, about women's role.

Some examples: The Taipings forbade foot binding and welcomed women members, establishing single-sex communities in which women were freed from family control and did useful work for the cause; they, as did the Boxers later, organized women into fighting groups, but these were brutally repressed. Reforms proposed in the 1890s included formal education for women and the abolition of foot binding, while utopian theorists proposed new ways of raising children and forms of egalitarian social relations. The Japanese schools for Chinese girls raised the revolutionary consciousness of future activists and gave them the skills to act politically. Thus Ch'iu Chin became a teacher in a Chinese women's school and plotted revolution with secret society members in the first decade of this century; the plan failed, and she was executed in 1907. There were reports of women in military units in the 1911 revolution, and women's suffrage groups emerged in the period of constitutional discussions in 1911–12. Several suffrage groups published in 1912 a parliamentary program calling for equal rights for men and women, education for women, improvement of their position in the family, monogamy, free choice of marriage partner, a ban on divorce without justification, an end to concubines and the sale of women, and reform of the licensed prostitution system. The attempt to work within the parliamentary system failed.

The discussion of women's rights was not hushed, however. The May 4 protest again brought women into popular politics and gender questions into the press. From Hunan, Mao Zedong wrote several articles on female suicide in 1919 that condemned the conditions (often a forced marriage) that drove women to suicide and urged them to struggle against the system instead of killing themselves in protest. Women students and teachers joined street crowds, read the new journals, and agitated in their own interests; they perceived women's rights as basic to a democratic society. In Hunan, a provincial constitution in 1922 granted women the suffrage in provincial and local elections. There the movement stopped, as warlordism and civil war engulfed the country.

Some of its members, however, went on to activism in the Communist party. One of them was Sister Shi, a Shanghai textile worker who joined a strike in 1922 and was recruited to the CCP; fired from her job, she ran a workers' school and was active in communist underground organizations. Xiang Jingyu, a Hunanese teacher, joined other young people in her province to sponsor a study group for workers; she was able to go to France to work and study communist ideas. She later was trained in Moscow as well, and organized women textile workers in China; the KMT executed her in 1928, during a wave of anticommunist repression. In rural Kwangtung, in areas where the economy had two bases—mulberry and silkworm cultivation, silk reeling and spinning, in which female workers predominated, and fishing, which employed primarily men—customs unknown in the rest of China occurred: Newlywed wives did not live with their husbands immediately, and young women refused to marry, organizing independent sisterhoods for social support.[100]

A second phase of research on Chinese women's history, done after the PRC permitted social scientists to interview people in villages and historians to explore archives, brought new studies closer to those done on other geographical areas. An example is Emily Honig's study of women in the Shanghai cotton mills from 1919 to 1949, which parallels those for Japan. Conditions were often similar to the Japanese (unscrupulous recruiters, crowded dormitory housing, poor wages and working conditions), but the Shanghai contract-labor system was not copied from the Japanese; instead, it was shaped by traditional Chinese labor recruitment practices. Women's experience as workers in Shanghai mills sometimes brought them into political struggles, as with Sister Shi and many other less-well-known women whose collective personal lives, wage-work patterns, and strikes are explored by Honig.[101]

An analysis of Japanese demographic records on Taiwan looks at gender relations, marriage, and childbearing, focusing on women in unconventional but socially accepted marriages. The marriages of adopted daughters raised as children with their future husbands were characterized both by much lower fertility and more frequent divorce. (These characteristics did not necessarily indicate better lives for these women, since both outcomes were highly stigmatized in the period.)[102] Gender relations in marriage and family are one of the most frequently addressed subjects of recent studies of China. Questions about the workings of the Confucian patriarchal system, the process by which it was reformed by law, the relationship between law (or tradition) and behavior, the extent to which socialist policy, with its commitment to gender equality and its belief that participation in social production is the driving force behind it, has succeeded, and the unintended or unanticipated consequences of other policies on gender and family relations have been widely discussed.

These historical studies explore new sources shedding light on gender and marriage in the past. A study of ritual guides, advice books, and commentary on marriage customs available to brides and their families in the late Qing period suggests that the possibilities for class-endogamous marriage were being undermined; one result was an intensified discourse about women as moral guardians of the family. The contractual differences in the price of, and expectations of services from, wives, concubines, and maids in the Hong Kong region in the early twentieth century trace a continuum rather than distinct breaks in status. An exploration of prostitution in Shanghai shows how women's bodies were commodified and made more accessible to men of all classes (previously concubinage was common primarily among elites). But even among prostitutes there were status differences, and perhaps more important, differences in what pay they might receive, what their conditions of work were, and what possibilities they had to leave the profession.

In 1907, in the waning years of the Qing, a revision of the Civil Code ended the right of the husband's family to control its daughters-in-law and introduced the notion of marriage as a contract between individuals. This was reinforced in the KMT 1930 Civil Code that prescribed freedom of marriage and facilitated divorce, but assumed that husbands had greater rights in marriage. Males continued to enjoy full authority over children, more grounds for divorce, and first claim to child custody. Any and all legal and institutional changes in these years were unevenly applied between rural and urban areas and among areas controlled by individual warlords or parties.[103]

During the Jiangxi Soviet, communists granted women new rights and sought their cooperation in replacing men as agricultural workers and as auxiliaries to the Red Army. The land law, for example, specified that landless laborers and peasants were to have equal rights to land portions regardless of sex. This law, which sought primarily to equalize property holding, not to emancipate women, gave class precedence over sex; hence landlords' wives shared their mates' class identity and were excluded from land redistribution. The two marriage laws (1931, 1934) promulgated in the Jiangxi Soviet followed USSR family law precedents. Marriage was defined as "free association between a man and a woman to be entered into without interference from other parties and to be ended by mutual agreement or upon the insistence of either husband or wife"; both marriage and divorce required official registration. There is little information about the implementation of these marriage laws, but some indication that the communists were uneasy about provoking male–female animosity.[104]

The marriage law of the PRC was drafted in 1949, before the civil war ended, and promulgated in 1950. Its principles echoed those of the 1931 law: free choice of partners, monogamy, equal rights of partners. The old customs—bigamy, concubinage, child betrothal, bride price, rejection of widow remarriage—were explicitly forbidden. Husbands and wives were declared equal in choice of occupation and activities, household status, the management of the household and its possessions, and their duty to work for the family's welfare. This marriage law was publicized, and efforts to enforce it started immediately, with uneven results; both private and official evasion continued in rural areas even as urban women flocked into wage work. Despite new legislation granting equal inheritance to males and females, the practice has not yet been accepted by rural families, who continue to disinherit daughters who marry out. The Women's Federation was created by the government to deal with some of these issues and promote women's interests. It accepted the party line that women should seek emancipation through social production and political activity, but also organized housewives.[105]

By the early 1980s, sociologists and anthropologists had more evidence about the effects of the marriage law, and their evaluation of it (reflecting the development of feminist theory) was less favorable. Judith Stacey argues that the revolution drew on patriarchy and compromised with it, producing a "new democratic patriarchy." The return to household-based agriculture and the one-child system suggested problems ahead. Margery Wolf's interviews (arranged by the government, as she emphasizes) in factories, schools, and neighborhood brigades put flesh and blood on the ideological–institutional sketch presented by Stacey. Wolf doubts any conscious intent of the revolutionaries to preserve patriarchy. Kay Johnson concludes, however, that "government policies have directly and indirectly supported the living dynamic of traditional values, behavior and family structure."[106]

Like France, the PRC has had long-standing demographic policies, but antinatalist rather than pronatalist ones. Chinese were told to marry late (women at eighteen or older), wait longer between births, and have fewer children. In the 1970s, even higher age minimums were aggressively pursued in administrative practice, and the 1979 one-child prescription was more forceful yet. The results: At the age-specific fertility rate prevailing in 1963 (an exceptionally prolific year), women would bear more than seven children in their lifetime on average; at 1985 rates, only slightly above two. This rapid achievement must be tempered, however, by the slowdown of rate of decline since 1980, and its partial reversal. The marriage law of that year raised the permissible age of marriage for women from eighteen to twenty, but administrative enforcement of higher age limits has been abandoned. The result has been increasingly young brides, at risk for childbearing for more years. Further, although rates of second and third births have declined, the relaxation of the one-child policy in rural areas has caused overall fertility to rise again there. It appears that marriage and childbearing policy, confronted by the return to household responsibility in agriculture (which might spur higher fertility in farm families seeking to ensure an adequate future workforce) has recently been undercut by lower ages at marriage.[107]

Feminist scholars have also been concerned by the effect on girl babies of the one-child policy; would agrarian parents who "needed" sons as family workers kill or neglect their daughters? There have been reports of such outcomes, but so far it has been hard to separate new effects from long-present trends. There is strong statistical evidence for Chinese female infanticide in the past, sometimes, but not always, linked to famine and crisis.[108]

China is one of the contemporary countries with a highly masculine sex ratio (1.074, compared to India's 1.066 or Pakistan's 1.105), attributed to higher female mortality rates at most ages from one to fifty or sixty. This phenomenon has received coverage in the popular press, but it, like its temporary historical parallel in European mortality statistics, is not fully understood.[109]

A recent review of Chinese women's position in the 1980s argues that the turbulent revolutionary years, despite their destruction and violence, gave young women a chance to escape from family control and develop new capabilities. The end of the GPCR narrowed such opportunities but did not silence debate about women's issues. New evidence from urban areas provides a unique and valuable summation of contemporary urban gender relations. Family structure in the cities changed rapidly after 1949; patrilocality withered away, and women's wage earning (and greater say in family spending and other decisions) became the norm. In the 1980s, divorce became more common, but as in the West, it is difficult for women to divorce because their wages are much lower than men's, and divorced women are stigmatized. The division of labor in the economy in the past decade appears to have sharpened sex segregation in jobs, with women in lower-paid and subordinate positions; this change is attributed to discrimination in work groups, which now are responsible for hiring. No government policy has been proposed to alleviate these outcomes. They, the continuing vulnerability of women to male violence, and increasing attention to beauty, dress, and adornment are officially condemned as feudal hangovers, the chaos of the GPCR, and Western influence. Both officials and ordinary people claim that the working out of socialist revolution will with time solve such problems, thus no special attention to them is needed. This seems unlikely, given the continuing resistance and government reluctance to enforce the laws. The Women's Federation has not taken an independent collective stand on most issues.

Under these conditions, Emily Honig and Gail Hershatter conclude that "women's subordination seem[s] certain to continue, if not by machination then by default."[110] This conclusion would be even more pessimistic if rural conditions are taken into account. Nevertheless, the continuing debate about women's status offers a glimmer of hope for the resumption of progress toward gender equality.

Conclusions and Agenda for Comparative Research

The comparisons made in this study confirm several generalizations: In most cases, early urbanization and industrialization probably decreased women's contribution to production overall, but the growth of the service sector made possible greater female contribution to the economy once more (the Chinese decision to promote export-oriented consumer industries may keep women in industry, however); government policy has been important not only to the organization of production, sectoral distribution, and division of labor in the economy as a whole but also to the division of labor and gender relations in the household; German and Japanese authoritarian government policies hindered gender realignment (the Chinese legislated gender equality and wavered on enforcement); among demographic factors, declining fertility and, in the West and Japan, reduced sex differentials in mortality among some female age groups made it possible for women to develop their capabilities through education and work; differences in forms of gender inequality both within states during the process of industrialization and between and among states at a given point in time were shaped by patterns of economic change, political stability, and government policies; variability in women's recourse to rights-based gender politics (especially social movements) was mediated by differences in political systems and power relations in regimes. Economic and political change in Britain first, then Western Europe and the United States, both offered a model for the rest of the world to emulate and had at least an indirect—and often a deleterious—impact on economic and political opportunities for non-Western men and women.

The improvements for men and women that followed industrialization, as well as variability in the forms of gender inequality among national states and within them across time and among social groups, have been summarized in each section. Here I would emphasize typical intergroup differences best documented for the West. For example, women in urban (excluding household production) and service industries (excluding domestic service) were better off economically than male day laborers in agriculture, and the wage gap between them and men in declining sectors such as household manufacturing and certain handicrafts was probably narrow as well. Middle-class women in social movements such as temperance, abolition, and suffrage were enjoying their capabilities more than most rural, immigrant, or racial-minority men were likely to. And rural, racial-minority, immigrant, and working-class women were less likely to benefit from urban and service-sector jobs (except those in domestic service) than their middle-class sisters. In the periods considered, women's capabilities compared to men's have varied with political and economic conditions, but despite positive increases in such capabilities as lower fertility, access to education and jobs, and political rights, gender inequality lingered. Continuing inequality in the household limited women's political and economic capabilities, preventing their full development.

Future research on the following questions would contribute to our understanding of the remaining problems. Did the discontinuities in wage inequality (improved female–male ratio in the move from agriculture to manufacturing, and from manufacturing to clerical work) that Claudia Goldin found in the United States occur in other countries? And do the same limits on improvements appear? (Here the role of large public-sector employment and the comparative impact of policies promoting or hindering wage equality seem critical.) To what extent would extending the period covered for Western countries to the welfare state and its greater intervention in women's access to jobs, social support policies, wages, education, and (to a lesser degree) household gender relations modify the picture of continuity within change? To what extent and through what mechanisms have public policies reduced gender inequality in households? To what extent can we historicize the concept of patriarchy, or are more-grounded concepts the prerequisite to systematic comparison seeking historical variation across political–economic systems? Under what conditions, and by what means, did men workers gain leverage to combine with employers at the expense of women workers? To what extent can we explain differences within specific feminist movements in their emphasis on workplace or family issues?

New research has greatly increased our knowledge about economic change and gender relations—in particular, the household and broader social divisions of labor by sex. This impressive record should encourage us to pursue the continuing agenda with optimism and energy.

NOTES

This essay was written while I was a fellow at the Center for Advanced Study in the Behavioral Sciences, Stanford, California. I am grateful for financial support provided by National Endowment for the Humanities #RA-20037-88, the Andrew W. Mellon Foundation, and the John Simon Guggenheim Memorial Foundation. Thanks also to Charles Tilly and Martin Whyte for reading the manuscript and making valuable suggestions for reorganization or revision.

1. Clara Collet, quoted in *Unequal Opportunities: Women's Employment in England 1800–1918*, ed. Angela John (Oxford, England: Basil Blackwell, 1986), p. 31.

2. Jeffrey G. Williamson, *Did British Capitalism Breed Inequality?* (Boston: Allen and Unwin, 1985), p. 200.

3. Claudia Goldin, *Understanding the Gender Gap: An Economic History of American Women* (New York: Oxford University Press, 1990).

4. For fuller discussion of Goldin's findings, see pp. 272–73.

5. Karen Oppenheim Mason, "The Status of Women: Conceptual and Methodological Issues in Demographic Studies," *Sociological Forum* 1 (Spring 1986): 284–300; and Sherry Ortner, "Gender Hegemonies," *Cultural Critique*, Winter 1989–90, pp. 35–81, both discuss the multidimensionality of women's prestige or status, male dominance, and the relative power of each sex and suggest alternative formulations to that adopted here.

6. Ivy Pinchbeck, *Women Workers and the Industrial Revolution, 1750–1850* (London: Virago, 1969; originally published 1930), p. 313.

7. Janet Thomas, "Women and Capitalism: Oppression or Emancipation? A Review Article," *Comparative Studies in Society and History* 30 (July 1988): 534–49, makes this point.

8. Edward Shorter, *The Making of the Modern Family* (New York: Basic Books, 1975), quote on p. 258.

9. Sonya O. Rose, " 'Gender at Work': Sex, Class and Industrial Capitalism," *History Workshop Journal* 21 (Spring 1986): 113–31; "Gender Segregation in the Transition to the Factory: The English Hosiery Industry, 1850–1910," *Feminist Studies* 13 (Spring 1987): 163–84; and "Gender Antagonism and Class Conflict: Exclusionary Strategies of Male Trade Unionists in Nineteenth-Century Britain," *Social History* 13 (May 1988): 191–230. See also Sonya Rose, *Limited Livelihoods: Gender and Class in Nineteenth-Century England* (Berkeley: University of California Press, 1992).

10. This essay is primarily written in a comparative history mode rather than with a global perspective; ideally it would be desirable to explore the global systemic connections among and between the cases considered.

11. In the introduction to their edited volume, *Women's Work and the Family Economy in Historical Perspective* (Manchester, England: Manchester University Press, 1991), Pat Hudson and W. R. Lee argue that women's experience in industrialization can best be approached through local or sectoral studies.

12. Amartya Sen, "Economics and the Family," *Asian Development Review* 1 (1983): 19. See also Jocelyn Kynch and Amartya Sen, "Indian Women: Well-Being and Survival," *Cambridge Journal of Economics* 7 (1983): 363–80. On p. 365 Sen develops his argument against utilitarian conceptions of pleasure and pain, John Rawls's position that individuals' advantage is based on their possession of widely desired goods like rights, liberties, opportunities, and wealth, and Ronald Dworkin's case for opportunities as the key to advantage. In "What Did you Learn in the World Today?" *American Behavioral Scientist* 34 (May–June 1991): 530–48,

Sen argues that equity (fairness in the distribution of "good things") should be given more weight in evaluating policy than efficiency (referring in part to having more "good things") and calls for disaggregated internal comparisons as well as cross-national aggregated ones in analyses of inequality.

13. Amartya Sen, "Gender and Cooperative Conflicts," in *Persistent Inequalities: Women and World Development*, ed. Irene Tinker, pp. 123–49 (New York: Oxford University Press, 1990), quote on p. 131; idem, "Economics and the Family," *Asian Development Review* 1 (1983), quote on p. 18.

14. The arenas in which capabilities are examined are not intended to suggest hierarchies of importance. These may vary from case to case, in different times or places. In the eighteenth and nineteenth centuries in the West, access to food and health care may have varied by gender; today it is effectively equal. In some parts of Asia and Africa today, however, such capabilities are still unequally distributed. See Kynch and Sen, "Indian Women," and Tim Dyson and Mick Moore, "On Kinship Structure, Female Autonomy, and Demographic Behavior in India," *Population and Development Review* 9 (March 1983): 35–60. Ray Langsten, "Determinants of High Female Mortality in South Asia: Are the Data Consistent with Theory?" has challenged the differential feeding hypothesis; his manuscript is discussed by Lillian Li, "Life and Death in a Chinese Famine: Infanticide as a Demographic Consequence of the 1935 Yellow River Flood," *Comparative Studies in Society and History* 33 (July 1991): 501.

15. Peter N. Stearns, *Interpreting the Industrial Revolution* (Washington, D.C.: American Historical Association, 1991). Revisions include C. K. Harley, "British Industrialization before 1841: Evidence of Slower Growth during the Industrial Revolution," *Journal of Economic History* 42 (1982): 267–89; Donald M. McCloskey, "The Industrial Revolution, 1780–1860," in *The Economic History of Britain since 1700*, ed. Roderick Floud and Donald M. McCloskey (Cambridge, England: Cambridge University Press, 1981); Rondo Cameron, "The Industrial Revolution: A Misnomer," *History Teacher* 15 (1982): 377–84, and "La revolution industrielle manquée," *Social Science History* 14 (1990): 559–65; see also the vigorous dissent by R. M. Hartwell, "Was There an Industrial Revolution?" *Social Science History* 14 (1990): 567–76; John Komlos, "Thinking about the Industrial Revolution," *Journal of European Economic History* 18 (1989): 191–206; Charles Sabel and Jonathan Zeitlin, "Historical Alternatives to Mass Production: Politics, Markets and Technology in Nineteenth-Century Industrialization," *Past and Present* 108 (August 1985): 132–76.

16. Chris Middleton, "Women's Labour and the Transition to Pre-Industrial Capitalism," in *Women and Work in Pre-Industrial England*, ed. Lindsey Charles and Lorna Duffin, pp. 181–206 (London: Croom Helm, 1985). See also the other case studies in this volume.

17. See the essays in Barbara A. Hanawalt, ed., *Women and Work in Preindustrial Europe* (Bloomington: Indiana University Press, 1986); and Susan Amussen, *An Ordered Society: Family and Village in England, 1560–1725* (Oxford, England: Basil Blackwell, 1988). The classic study is Alice Clark, *The Working Life of Women in the Seventeenth Century* (New York: Routledge, 1982).

18. For an early statement of the "protoindustrial thesis," see Franklin F.

Mendels, "Proto-industrialization: The First Phase in the Industrialization Process," *Journal of Economic History* 32 (1972): 241–61; Hans Medick, "The Proto-Industrial Family Economy: The Structural Function of Household and Family during the Transition from Peasant Society to Industrial Capitalism," *Social History* 3 (1976): 291–315. See also David Levine, *Family Formation in an Age of Nascent Capitalism* (New York: Academic Press, 1977); and idem, "Industrialization and the Proletarian Family in England," *Past and Present* 107 (1985): 168–203. Both Middleton, "Women's Labour," and Maxine Berg, "Women's Work, Mechanization and the Early Phases of Industrialization in England," *On Work: Historical, Comparative, and Theoretical Approaches*, ed. R. E. Pahl, pp. 61–94 (New York and Oxford, England: Basil Blackwell, 1988) see protoindustrialization as more oppressive than do Medick and Levine. The latter's position on the demographic correlates of protoindustrialization is also challenged by Richard M. Smith, "Putting the Child Before the Marriage: Reply to Birdsall," *Population and Development Review* 9 (1983), 124–36; and, for France, by Pierre Jeannin, "La protoindustrialisation: developpement ou impasse?" *Annales: Économies, Sociétés, Civilisations* 35 (1980): 52–65. In their *Population History of England, 1541–1871* (Cambridge, Mass.: Harvard University Press, 1981), E. A. Wrigley and Roger Schofield show that women's childbearing and household responsibilities increased in the period of protoindustrialization, although they attribute higher fertility to better real wages, not the spread of the new organization of production. David Gaunt has labeled this increased fertility the "demographic background to woman as the beast of burden in the Industrial Revolution." See Gaunt's contribution to "The Population History of England 1541–1871: A Review Symposium," *Social History* 8 (1983): 139–68. For critiques of the protoindustrialization literature that emphasize the proletarianization of urban crafts, see Maxine Berg, Pat Hudson, and Michael Sonenscher, *Manufacture in Town and Country before the Factory* (Cambridge, England: Cambridge University Press, 1983).

19. K.D.M. Snell, *Annals of the Labouring Poor: Social Change in Agrarian England, 1660–1900* (Cambridge, England: Cambridge University Press, 1985), quote on p. 311.

20. Edward Higgs, "Domestic Service and Household Production," in John, *Unequal Opportunities*, pp. 125–50. For an overview (based on census aggregates) of patterns of servant employment in English middle-class households, see Patricia Branca, *Silent Sisterhood: Middle-Class Women in the Victorian Home* (London: Croom Helm, 1975).

21. Berg, "Women's Work, Mechanization." The heavy employment of children in the factory-organized cotton industry attracted the attention of reformers. Although child labor was declining, laws were passed in the nineteenth century to protect child workers. The first effective Factory Act (1833) extended the age of protected workers to eighteen, provided for inspectors, and required factory owners to establish schools for their workers under age thirteen. Women were added to the protected groups in an 1844 amendment. Cotton textile workers opposed the elimination of half-timers (children who both attended school and worked in the factories) well into the twentieth century, resisting both Trades Union Congress policy and the notion of a primary male breadwinner in the interests of their family

economies. Per Bolin-Hort, *Work, Family and the State: Child Labour and the Organization of Production in the British Cotton Industry, 1780–1920* (Lund, Sweden: Lund University Press, 1989). See also Margaret Hewitt, *Wives and Mothers in Victorian Industry* (Westport, Conn.: Greenwood Press, 1975; originally published 1958).

"Family wage" referred also to a wage adequate to support a family, a concept the implementation of which male craftsmen and some unionists urged through laws limiting women's access to jobs and prohibiting married women's wage work. See Sheila Lewenhak, *Women and Trade Unions* (New York: St. Martin's Press, 1977); and Barbara Drake, *Women in Trade Unions* (London: Virago, 1984). In "The Working Class Family, Women's Liberation and Class Struggle: The Case of Nineteenth Century British History," *Review of Radical Political Economics* 9 (Fall 1977): 25–41 and "Class Struggle and the Persistence of the Working Class Family," *Cambridge Journal of Economics* 1 (1977): 241–58, Jane Humphries argues that the family wage was a tactic to preserve the working-class family and support its reproductive capacities by improving its standard of living through class struggle. See also Harold Benenson, "The 'Family Wage' and Working Women's Consciousness in Britain, 1880–1914," *Politics and Society* 19 (March 1991): 71–108, who shows that many women cotton textile workers opposed any "marriage bar" or protective legislation that limited their access to jobs; and Mariana Valverde, " 'Giving the Female a Domestic Turn': The Social, Legal and Moral Regulation of Women's Work in British Cotton Mills, 1820–1850," *Journal of Social History* 21 (1988): 619–34, who shows that male workers' opinions on this issue changed over time, and they eventually settled not for exclusion but the marginalization of women in factories. The proportion of women working did not decline despite the discourse of domesticity.

22. Angela John, discussing Jenny Morris, "The Characteristics of Sweating: The Late Nineteenth-Century London and Leeds Tailoring Trade," in John, *Unequal Opportunities*, p. 11. John's volume was published at the same time as Jane Lewis, ed., *Labor and Love: Women's Experience of Home and Family, 1850–1940* (New York and Oxford, England: Basil Blackwell, 1986); the two collections were conceptualized to cover two aspects of gender relations: those in the workplace (John) and those in the home (Lewis).

23. Judith Lown, *Women and Industrialization: Gender at Work in Nineteenth-Century England* (Minneapolis: University of Minnesota Press, 1990).

24. Marguerite Dupree, "The Community Perspective in Family History: The Potteries during the Nineteenth Century," in *The First Modern Society: Essays in English History in Honour of Lawrence Stone*, ed. A. L. Beier, David Canadine, and James M. Rosenheim, pp. 549–73 (Cambridge, England: Cambridge University Press, 1989). Dupree's focus on Stoke-upon-Trent provides the opportunity to compare two labor markets—those of ceramics workers and coal miners—and their social context in one setting. Richard Whipp, "Kinship, Labour and Enterprise: The Staffordshire Pottery Industry, 1890–1920," in Hudson and Lee, *Women's Work*, pp. 184–203.

25. Angela V. John, *By the Sweat of Their Brow: Women Workers at Victorian Coal Mines* (Boston: Routledge and Kegan Paul, 1984).

26. Elizabeth A. M. Roberts, "Women's Strategies, 1890–1940," in Lewis, *Labor and Love*, pp. 223–47; and *Women's Work 1840–1940* (London: Macmillan

Education, 1988). See also John Benson, *The Penny Capitalists: A Study of Nineteenth-Century Working-Class Entrepreneurs* (New Brunswick, N.J.: Rutgers University Press, 1983), which gives most attention to male enterprises; and Diana Gittins, "Marital Status, Work and Kinship, 1850–1930," and L. Jamieson, "Limited Resources and Limiting Conventions," both in Lewis, *Labor and Love*; Carl Chinn, *They Worked All Their Lives: Women of the Urban Poor in England, 1880–1939* (New York: Manchester University Press, 1988).

27. Pat Ayers and Jan Lambertz, "Marriage Relations, Money, and Domestic Violence in Working-Class Liverpool, 1919–1939," in Lewis, *Labour and Love*, pp. 195–219. A strict division of household responsibility was also reported in mining families; see Norman Dennis, Fernando Henriques and Clifford Slaughter, *Coal Is Our Life: An Analysis of a Yorkshire Mining Community* (London: Eyre & Spottiswoode, 1956). On working-class wives' health and diets, see Jane Lewis, *The Politics of Motherhood: Child and Maternal Welfare in England, 1900–1939* (London: Croom Helm, 1980); and John Komlos, "Anthropometric History: What Is It?" *Journal of Social and Biological Structures* 14 (1991): 353–56, which cites several gender-specific studies that connect height differences by gender to women's malnutrition. For studies of working-class married life in London, see Ellen Ross, " 'Fierce Questions and Taunts': Married Life in Working Class London," *Feminist Studies* 8 (1982): 575–602, and "Survival Networks: Women's Neighborhood Sharing in London before World War One," *History Workshop Journal* 15 (1983): 4–27. See also Wally Seccombe, "Patriarchy Stabilized: The Construction of the Male Breadwinner Wage Norm in Nineteenth-Century Britain," *Social History* 11 (January 1986): 53–76; and Wally Seccombe, *A Millenium of Family Change: Feudalism to Capitalism in Northwestern Europe* (London: Verso, 1992).

28. Michael Anderson, "The Emergence of the Modern Life Cycle in Britain," *Social History* 10 (January 1985): 69–87; Ellen Jordan, "The Exclusion of Women from Industry in Nineteenth-Century Britain," *Comparative Studies in Society and History* 31 (April 1989): 273–96; Wrigley and Schofield, *Population History of England*.

29. Levine, "Industrialization and the Proletarian Family." To those who would associate declining fertility with the spread of education, Levine points out that the "introduction of mass education *followed* the working-class family's recomposition; it did not precede it" (p. 195).

30. S. Ryan Johansson, "Welfare, Mortality and Gender: Continuity and Change in the Explanation of Male/Female Mortality Differences over Three Centuries," *Continuity and Change* 6 (1991): 135–77. See also Roger Schofield, "Did the Mothers Really Die? Three Centuries of Maternal Mortality in the World We Have Lost," in *The World We Have Gained: Histories of Population and Social Structure*, ed. Lloyd Bonfield, Richard M. Smith, and Keith Wrightson, pp. 231–60 (New York: Oxford University Press, 1986).

31. Leonore Davidoff and Catherine Hall, *Family Fortunes: Men and Women of the English Middle Class, 1780–1850* (Chicago: University of Chicago Press, 1987), quotes on pp. 12, 25; Anne Summers, "A Home from Home—Women's Philanthropic Work in the Nineteenth Century," in *Fit Work for Women*, ed. Sandra Burman, pp. 32–63 (New York: St. Martin's Press, 1979).

32. Catherine Hall, "Strains in the 'Firm of Wife, Children and Friends'? Middle Class Women and Employment in Early Nineteenth-Century England," in Hudson and Lee, *Women's Work*, pp. 106–31.

33. Lee Holcombe, *Victorian Ladies at Work: Middle-Class Working Women in England and Wales, 1850–1914* (New York: Archon Books, 1973), and *Wives and Property: Reform of Married Women's Property Law in Nineteenth-Century England* (Toronto: University of Toronto Press, 1983); Mary Lyndon Shanley, *Feminism, Marriage, and the Law in Victorian England, 1850–1895* (Princeton: Princeton University Press, 1989); Samuel Cohn, *The Process of Occupational Sex-Typing: The Feminization of Clerical Labor in Great Britain* (Philadelphia: Temple University Press, 1989); Meta Zimmeck, "Clerical Work for Women, 1850–1914," in John, *Unequal Opportunities*, pp. 153–77. See also Dina M. Copelman, " 'A New Comradeship between Men and Women': Family, Marriage and London's Women Teachers, 1870–1914," in Lewis, *Labour and Love*, pp. 175–93, for discussion of the continued participation of wives in small business and commerce and of the willingness of more prosperous working-class and lower-middle-class families to forego daughters' financial contribution to prepare them for better jobs, such as school teaching.

34. Jane Rendall, ed., *Equal or Different: Women's Politics, 1800–1914* (Oxford, England: Basil Blackwell, 1987), and *The Origins of Modern Feminism: Women in Britain, France and the United States, 1780–1860* (Chicago: Lyceum, 1985); Jill Liddington and Jill Norris, *One Hand Tied Behind Us: The Rise of the Women's Suffrage Movement* (London: Virago, 1978).

35. Judith R. Walkowitz, *Prostitution and Victorian Society: Women, Class, and the State* (Cambridge, England: Cambridge University Press, 1980); Patricia Hollis, *Ladies Elect: Women in English Local Government, 1865–1914* (Oxford, England: Clarendon Press, 1987); Rendall, *Equal or Different* and *The Origins*; Seth Koven and Sonya Michel, "Womanly Duties: Maternalist Politics and the Origins of Welfare States in France, Germany, Great Britain, and the United States, 1880–1920," *American Historical Review* 95 (October 1990): 1076–1108.

36. Jane Jenson argues in "Gender and Reproduction: Or, Babies and the State," *Studies in Political Economy* 20 (Summer 1986): 9–46, that the British politics of motherhood restricted women's access to jobs while the French offered ways to balance wage work and domestic roles. Ellen Mappen, *Helping Women at Work: The Women's Industrial Council, 1889–1914* (London: Hutchinson, 1985) shows that some social feminists were conscious of this problem and despite sometimes contradictory ideology and practice initiated local projects to support women workers who were mothers.

37. See Barbara F. Reskin and Patricia A. Roos, *Job Queues, Gender Queues: Explaining Women's Inroads into Male Occupations* (Philadelphia: Temple University Press, 1990), for discussion of similar processes in the contemporary United States.

38. See Alan S. Milward and S. B. Saul, *The Economic Development of Continental Europe, 1780–1870* (Totawa, N.J.: Rowan and Littlefield, 1973), for a description of the French economy in European perspective.

39. François Crouzet, "Angleterre et France au XVIIIe siècle: Essai d'analyse comparée de deux croissances économiques," *Annales: Economies, Sociétés, Civilisations* 21 (March–April 1966): 254–91.

40. Olwen Hufton, *The Poor of Eighteenth-Century France* (Oxford, England: Clarendon Press, 1974), and "Women and the Family Economy in Eighteenth-Century France," *French Historical Studies* 9 (1975): 7–22; Jeffrey Kaplow, *Elbeuf during the Revolutionary Period* (Baltimore: Johns Hopkins University Press, 1964), and *The Names of Kings: The Parisian Laboring Poor in the Eighteenth Century* (New York: Basic Books, 1972).

41. Gay Gullickson's study of protoindustry in the Pays de Caux (Normandy) in the eighteenth and nineteenth centuries challenges some of the original generalizations about protoindustrialization as explicated by Franklin Mendels, Hans Medick, and David Levine (see note 17). She shows that protoindustry in the Caux involved a gender division of labor (with men in commercial agriculture and women weaving) rather than a family economy with all members in a single industry. Gullickson, *Spinners and Weavers of Auffay: Rural Industry and the Sexual Division of Labor in a French Village, 1750–1850* (Cambridge, England: Cambridge University Press, 1986). See also Tessie Liu, *The Weavers' Knot: The Contradictions of Class Struggle and Family Solidarity in Western France, 1750–1914* (Ithaca, N.Y.: Cornell University Press, 1994).

42. Martine Segalen, "Exploring a Case of Late French Fertility Decline: Two Contrasted Breton Examples," in *The European Experience of Declining Fertility: A Quiet Revolution, 1850–1970*, ed. John Gillis, Louise A. Tilly, and David Levine (Oxford, England: Basil Blackwell, 1992); Etienne van de Walle, *The Female Population of France in the Nineteenth Century: A Reconstruction of 82 Departments* (Princeton: Princeton University Press, 1974), and "Motivations and Technology in the Decline of French Fertility," in *Family and Sexuality in French History*, ed. Tamara Hareven and Robert Wheaton, pp. 135–78 (Philadelphia: University of Pennsylvania Press, 1980).

43. Martine Segalen, *Love and Power in the Peasant Family: Rural France in the Nineteenth Century* (Chicago: University of Chicago Press, 1983), quote on p. 9.

44. Gender relations in Languedocian vineyards and winegrowing are discussed in Laura Frader, "Grapes of Wrath: Vineyard Workers, Labor Unions, and Strike Activity in the Aude, 1860–1913," in *Class Conflict and Collective Action*, ed. Louise A. Tilly and Charles Tilly, pp. 185–206 (Beverly Hills: Sage, 1981). According to Paul Bairoch, "Niveaux de developpement économique de 1810 à 1910," *Annales: Economies, Sociétés, Civilisations* 20 (November–December 1965): 1096, the relatively small scale of French agriculture meant that in 1910, according to an index comparing levels of agricultural development (in terms of productivity) across nations, France came in well behind the United States, Britain, and Germany but well ahead of Russia, the Mediterranean countries, and Japan. Adna Ferrin Weber, *The Growth of Cities in the Nineteenth Century* (Ithaca, N.Y.: Cornell University Press, 1967), shows that while 79 percent of the French population lived outside cities of over 20,000 in 1891, only 41 percent of the English population did (p. 144).

45. Louise A. Tilly, "Individual Lives and Family Strategies in the French Proletariat," *Journal of Family History* 4 (Summer 1979): 137–52; idem, "The Family Wage Economy of a French Textile City: Roubaix, 1872–1906," *Journal of Family History* 4 (Winter 1979): 381–94; idem, "Linen Was Their Life: Family Strategies and Parent–Child Relations in Nineteenth-Century France," in *Interest and Emo-*

57

tion: Essays on the Study of Family and Kinship, ed. Hans Medick and David Warren Sabean, pp. 300–316 (Cambridge, England: Cambridge University Press, 1984); and idem, "Worker Families and Occupation in Industrial France," *Tocqueville Review* 5 (Fall–Winter, 1983): 317–36.

46. John M. Merriman, *The Red City: Limoges and the French Nineteenth Century* (New York: Oxford University Press, 1985).

47. Michelle Perrot, *Les Ouvriers en Grève: France, 1871–1890* (Paris and The Hague: Mouton, 1974). See also Louise A. Tilly, "Paths of Proletarianization: The Sex Division of Labor and Women's Collective Action in Nineteenth-Century France," *Signs: Journal of Women in Culture and Society* 7 (Winter 1981): 400–417, and "Coping with Company Paternalism: Family Strategies of Coal Miners in Nineteenth-Century France," *Theory and Society* 14 (July 1985): 403–17.

48. Joan Wallach Scott, "Men and Women in the Parisian Garment Trades: Discussions of Family and Work in the 1830s and 1840s," in *The Power of the Past: Essays for Eric Hobsbawm*, ed. Pat Tháne, Geoff Crossick, and Roderick Floud, pp. 69–73 (Cambridge, England: Cambridge University Press, 1984); Marilyn J. Boxer, "Women in Industrial Home Work: The Flowermakers of Paris in the Belle Epoque," *French Historical Studies* 22 (1982): 401–23, and "Protective Legislation and Home Industry: The Marginalization of Women Workers in Late Nineteenth-Early Twentieth-Century France," *Journal of Social History* 20 (1986): 45–65; Judith Coffin, "Social Science Meets Sweated Labor: Reinterpreting Women's Work in Late Nineteenth-Century France," *Journal of Modern History* 63 (June 1991): 230–70.

49. Marie-Helène Zylberberg-Hocquard, "Les ouvrières de l'État (Tabacs et Alumettes) dans les dernières années du XIXe siècle," *Le Mouvement social* 105 (October–December, 1978): 87–108.

50. Theresa M. McBride, "A Woman's World: Department Stores and the Evolution of Women's Employment, 1870–1920," *French Historical Studies* 20 (Fall 1978): 664–83; Susan Bachrach, *Dames Employées: The Feminization of Postal Work in Nineteenth-Century France* (New York: Institute for Research in History/Haworth, 1984); Frances I. Clark, *The Position of Women in Contemporary France* (Westport, Conn.: Hyperion Press, 1981; originally published 1937); see also Michelle Perrot's introduction (which opens with the words "Women have always worked. They have not always had métiers") and the other articles in *Le Mouvement social* cited in note 49. See also Jo Burr Margadant, *Madame Le Professeur: Women Educators in the Third Republic* (Princeton: Princeton University Press, 1990).

51. For further comparisons of France and England, see Louise A. Tilly and Joan W. Scott, *Women, Work and Family*, 2nd ed. (New York: Methuen, 1987).

52. Louise A. Tilly, "Occupational Structure, Women's Work and Demographic Change in Two French Industrial Cities, Anzin and Roubaix, 1872–1906," in *Time, Space and Man*, ed. Jan Sundin and Erik Söderlund (Atlantic Highlands, N.J.: Humanities Press, 1979), and "Individual Lives and Family Strategies in the French Proletariat," *Journal of Family History* 4 (Summer 1979): 137–52.

53. See Jacques Caroux-Destray, *Une Famille ouvrière traditionnelle* (Paris: Anthropos, 1974); Henry Leyret, *En Plein faubourg: moeurs ouvrières* (Paris: Charpentier, 1895), esp. pp. 49–50, 122.

54. Bonnie G. Smith, *Ladies of the Leisure Class: The Bourgeoises of Northern France in the Nineteenth Century* (Princeton: Princeton University Press, 1981).

55. For the 1789–95 revolutionary period, see Harriet Applewhite and Darlene Levy, eds., *Women and Politics in the Age of the Democratic Revolution* (Ann Arbor: University of Michigan Press, 1990); Louise A. Tilly, "Women's Collective Action and Feminism in France, 1870–1914," in *Class Conflict and Collective Action*, ed. Louise A. Tilly and Charles Tilly, pp. 207–31 (Beverly Hills: Sage, 1981); Karen O. Offen, "The 'Woman Question' as a Social Issue in Nineteenth-Century France," *Third Republic/Troisième République* 3–4 (1977): 238–99, "Depopulation, Nationalism and Feminism in Fin-de-siècle France," *American Historical Review* 89 (June 1984): 648–76, and "Defining Feminism: A Comparative Historical Approach," *Signs: Journal of Women in Culture and Society* 14 (Autumn 1988): 119–57; Steven C. Hause and Anne R. Kenney, *Women's Suffrage and Social Politics in the French Third Republic* (Princeton: Princeton University Press, 1984); Miriam Cohen and Michael Hanagan, "The Politics of Gender and the Making of the Welfare State, 1900–1940: A Comparative Perspective," *Journal of Social History* 24 (1991): 469–84; Jenson, "Gender and Reproduction"; Peter Flora and Arnold J. Heidenheimer, *The Development of Welfare States in Europe and America* (New Brunswick, N.J.: Rutgers University Press, 1987); Mary Lynn Stewart, *Women, Work, and the French State* (Montreal: McGill–Queens University Press, 1989).

56. Patricia Hilden, *Working Women and Socialist Politics in France, 1880–1914: A Regional Study* (Oxford, England: Clarendon Press, 1986); Marilyn J. Boxer and Jean H. Quataert, eds., *Socialist Women: European Socialist Feminism in the Nineteenth and Early Twentieth Centuries* (New York: Elsevier, 1978); Charles Sowerwine, *Sisters or Citizens? Women and Socialism in France Since 1876* (Cambridge, England: Cambridge University Press, 1982); Maité Albistur and Daniel Armogathe, *Histoire du féminisme français du moyen âge à nos jours* (Paris: Editions des femmes, 1977).

57. Its territory then encompassed regions now in France, Belgium, Poland, Lithuania, Czechoslovakia, and Denmark. Before that, it was an amalgam of smaller states; when I speak of them collectively, I use the word Germany, but when I speak of a specific area, I either identify it geographically or use the name of the state then in control. Milward and Saul, *Economic Development*, is the source for the economic history that follows.

58. Jean H. Quataert, "The Shaping of Women's Work in Manufacturing: Guilds, Households, and the State in Central Europe, 1648–1870," *American Historical Review* 90 (December 1985): 1122–48.

59. Peter Kriedte, Hans Medick, and Jürgen Schlumbohm, *Industrialization before Industrialization: Rural Industry in the Genesis of Capitalism* (Cambridge, England: Cambridge University Press, 1981).

60. Milward and Saul, *Economic Development*, pp. 304, 371, 383–84.

61. W. R. Lee, "Women's Work and the Family: Some Demographic Implications of Gender-Specific Rural Work Patterns in Nineteenth-Century Germany," in Hudson and Lee, *Working Women*, pp. 50–75; and Arthur E. Imhof, "Women, Family and Death: Excess Mortality of Women in Childbearing Age in Four Communities in Nineteenth-Century Germany," in *The German Family in Nineteenth- and Twentieth-Century Germany*, ed. Richard Evans and W. R. Lee, pp. 148–74 (London:

Croom Helm, 1981). See also David Sabean's study of a Württemberg community, *Property, Production and Family in Neckarhausen, 1700–1870* (Cambridge, England: Cambridge University Press, 1990), for discussion of women's heavy labor in stall feeding and the increased family conflict, nonmarriage, and illegitimacy that occurred in this period in Neckarhausen. Note that the German evidence about the intensification of women's agricultural labor offers a distinct contrast to Snell's findings (*Annals of Labor*) in southeastern England and to Johansson's use of Snell's conclusion to explain nineteenth-century elevated death rates among English adolescents and young women.

62. John Knodel, *The Decline of Fertility in Germany, 1871–1939* (Princeton: Princeton University Press, 1974); Milward and Saul, *Economic Development*, pp. 131–32.

63. Barbara Franzoi, *At the Very Least She Pays the Rent: Women and German Industrialization, 1871–1914* (Westport, Conn.: Greenwood Press, 1985).

64. Kathleen Canning, "Gender and The Politics of Class Formation: Rethinking German Labor History," *American Historical Review* 97 (1992): 736–68, offers a sensitive picture of women textile workers. Case studies of workers in German cities dominated by heavy industry reveal the near nonexistence of jobs for women workers and their almost total absence from workers' organizations or socialist politics. See David F. Crew, *Town in the Ruhr: A Social History of Bochum, 1860–1914* (New York: Columbia University Press, 1979); and Mary Nolan, *Social Democracy and Society: Working-class Radicalism in Dusseldorf* (Cambridge, England: Cambridge University Press, 1981).

65. Robyn Dasey, "Women's Work and the Family: Women Garment Workers in Berlin and Hamburg Before the First World War," in Evans and Lee, *The German Family*, pp. 221–55; Katharina Schlegal, "Mistress and Servant in Nineteenth Century Hamburg: Employer/Employee Relationships in Domestic Service, 1880–1914," *History Workshop Journal* 15 (Spring 1983): 60–77; Mary Jo Maynes, "The Contours of Childhood: Demography, Strategy, and Mythology of Childhood in French and German Lower-Class Autobiographies," in *The European Experience of Declining Fertility, 1850–1970: The Quiet Revolution*, ed. John R. Gillis, Louise A. Tilly, and David Levine, pp. 101–24 (Cambridge, Mass.: Blackwell, 1992); Jean H. Quataert, "Social Insurance and the Family Work of Oberlausitz Home Weavers in the Late Nineteenth Century," in *German Women in the Nineteenth Century: A Social History*, ed. John C. Fout, pp. 270–94 (New York: Holmes and Meier, 1984), uses evidence from government investigations and appeals in pension cases to show that women weavers were often denied pensions—despite the 1894 law extending them to hand weavers—because they were considered to be assistants to their husbands (this even though their husbands by this period were likely to be only part-time weavers, with construction or other seasonal jobs elsewhere). Quataert argues that families were complicit in this misrepresentation because they were unable or unwilling to pay the required contribution to the pension plan for two members of the household.

66. Carole J. Adams, *Women Clerks in Wilhelmine Germany: Issues of Class and Gender* (Cambridge, England: Cambridge University Press, 1989).

67. Mary Jo Maynes, *Schooling for the People: Comparative Local Studies on*

Schooling History in France and Germany, 1750–1850 (New York: Holmes and Meier, 1985), and *Schooling in Western Europe: A Social History* (Albany: SUNY Press, 1985).

68. Frederick Engels, *The Origin of the Family, Private Property and the State* (New York: International Publishers, 1942; originally published 1884); Jean Quataert, *Reluctant Feminists in German Social Democracy, 1885–1917* (Princeton: Princeton University Press, 1979); Amy Hackett, "The German Women's Movement and Suffrage, 1890–1914: A Study of National Feminism," in Robert J. Bezucha, *Modern European Social History*, pp. 354–79 (Lexington, Mass.: D.C. Heath, 1972); see also Richard J. Evans, *The Feminist Movement in Germany, 1894–1933* (London: Croom Helm, 1976).

69. Thomas Dublin, *Women at Work: The Transformation of Work and Community in Lowell, Massachusetts (1826–1860)* (New York: Columbia University Press, 1981), and *Farm and Factory: The Mill Experience and Women's Lives in New England, 1830–1860* (New York: Columbia University Press, 1981). Evidence collected by Claudia Goldin and Kenneth Sokoloff, "Women, Children, and Industrialization in the Early Republic: Evidence from the Manufacturing Censuses," *Journal of Economic History* 42 (December 1982): 741–74, shows that the ratio of female to male full-time wages was higher in manufacturing. See also Lucy Simler, "The Landless Worker: An Index of Economic and Social Change in Chester County, Pa., 1750–1820," *Pennsylvania Magazine of History and Biography* 114 (April 1990): esp. 185–87, for evidence of equal wages paid to men and women agricultural workers; Goldin, *Understanding the Gender Gap*, pp. 59–68; and Alice Kessler-Harris, *Out to Work: A History of Wage-Earning Women in the United States* (New York: Oxford University Press, 1982). See also Thomas Dublin, "Women's Work and the Family Economy: Textiles and Palm Leaf Hatmaking in New England, 1830–1850," *Tocqueville Review* 5 (Fall–Winter 1983): 297–316, and "Rural Putting-Out Work in Early Nineteenth-Century New England: Women and the Transition to Capitalism in the Countryside," *New England Quarterly* (1991): 531–73. Jeanne Boydston, *Home and Work: Housework, Wages and the Ideology of Labor in the Early Republic* (New York: Oxford University Press, 1990), examines the conditions under which housework lost both visibility and value with the rise of market relations; she argues that the process became the prototype for the "restructuring of the social relations of labor under . . . early industrialization" (p. xx). Tamara Hareven, *Family Time and Industrial Time* (Cambridge, England: Cambridge University Press, 1982), carries the story of the cotton industry, its immigrant workers, and their families into the twentieth century with a study of the world's largest textile mill. The Amoskeag Company in Manchester, Massachusetts, failed in the 1920s as the industry pursued a new low-wage strategy—moving to the job-hungry South. Jacqueline Dowd Hall et al., *Like a Family* (New York: Norton, 1989), partially based on oral history, as is Hareven's study, examines the conditions of textile work and family in North Carolina in the first decades of this century; race as well as gender and class are factors in this history.

70. Mary H. Blewett, *Men, Women, and Work: Class, Gender, and Protest in the New England Shoe Industry, 1780–1910* (Urbana: University of Illinois Press, 1987).

71. Christine Stansell, *City of Women: Sex and Class in New York, 1789–1860* (New York: Knopf, 1986), offers a complex and nuanced picture of gender relations

in the metropolis; James Oliver Horton, "Freedom's Yoke: Gender Conventions among Antebellum Free Blacks," *Feminist Studies* 22 (Spring 1986): 51–76; and Suzanne Lebsock, *The Free Women of Petersburg: Status and Culture in a Southern Town, 1784–1860* (New York: Norton, 1984), look at free African American women in the North and South.

72. Carole Turbin, "And We Are Nothing but Women: Irish Working Women in Troy," in *Women in America: A History*, ed. Carol R. Berkin and Mary Beth Norton (New York: Houghton Mifflin, 1979), and "Beyond Conventional Wisdom: Women's Wage Work, Household Economic Contribution, and Labor Activism in a Mid-Nineteenth-Century Working-Class Community," in *"To Toil the Livelong Day": America's Women at Work, 1780–1980*, ed. Carol Groneman and Mary Beth Norton, pp. 47–83 (Ithaca, N.Y.: Cornell University Press, 1987).

73. Ava Baron, "Contested Terrain Revisited: Technology and Gender Definitions of Work in the Printing Industry, 1850–1920," in *Women, Work, and Technology: Transformations*, ed. Barbara Wright (Ann Arbor: University of Michigan Press, 1987); Ava Baron, "Questions of Gender: Deskilling and Demasculinization in the U.S. Printing Industry, 1830–1915," *Gender and History* 1 (Summer 1989): 178–99; and Ava Baron, "An 'Other' Side of Gender Antagonism at Work: Men, Boys, and the Remasculinization of Printers' Work, 1830–1920," in *Work Engendered: Toward a New History of American Labor*, ed. Ava Baron (Ithaca, N.Y.: Cornell University Press, 1991).

74. Daniel J. Walkowitz, *Worker City, Company Town: Iron and Cotton Worker Protest in Troy and Cohoes, New York, 1855–1884* (Urbana: University of Illinois Press, 1978); S. J. Kleinberg, *The Shadow of the Mills: Working-Class Families in Pittsburgh, 1870–1907* (Pittsburgh: University of Pittsburgh Press, 1989). On Pittsburgh, see also John Bodnar, *Workers' World: Kinship, Community, and Protest in an Industrial Society, 1900–1940* (Baltimore: Johns Hopkins University Press, 1982); and John Bodnar, Roger Simon, and Michael P. Weber, *Lives of Their Own: Blacks, Italians, and Poles in Pittsburgh, 1900–1960* (Urbana: University of Illinois Press, 1982). On New York, see Donna Gabaccia, *From Sicily to Elizabeth Street: Housing and Social Change Among Italian Immigrants, 1880–1930* (Albany: SUNY Press, 1984); and Miriam Cohen, *From Workshop to Office: Employment, School and Family in the Lives of New York Italian Women, 1900–1950* (Ithaca, N.Y.: Cornell University Press, 1993). Elizabeth Pleck, "A Mother's Wages: A Comparison of Income-Earning among Married Black and Italian Women, 1896–1911," in *A Heritage of Her Own: Toward a New Social History of American Women*, ed. Nancy F. Cott and Elizabeth Pleck, pp. 367–92 (New York: Simon and Schuster, 1979), compares African American and Italian women in several cities.

75. Dolores Janiewski, "Seeking 'a New Day and a New Way': Black Women and Unions in the Southern Tobacco Industry," in Groneman and Norton, '*To Toil the Livelong Day*,' pp. 161–78; and Dolores E. Janiewski, *Sisterhood Denied: Race, Gender and Class in a New South Community* (Philadelphia: Temple University Press, 1985); Jacqueline Jones, "The Political Implications of Black and White Women's Work in the South, 1890–1965," and Nancy Hewitt, "Varieties of Voluntarism: Class, Ethnicity, and Women's Activism in Tampa," both in *Women, Politics, and Change*, ed. Louise A. Tilly and Patricia Gurin, pp. 108–29, 63–86 (New York:

Russell Sage Foundation, 1990); Jacqueline Jones, *Labor of Love, Labor of Sorrow, Black Women, Work and the Family from Slavery to the Present* (New York: Basic Books, 1985); and Patricia A. Cooper, *Once a Cigar Maker: Men, Women, and Work Culture in American Cigar Factories, 1900–1919* (Urbana: University of Illinois Press, 1987). See also the case studies in Baron, *Work Engendered*, for specific industries and localities.

76. Ardis Cameron, "Bread and Roses Revisited: Women's Culture and Working-Class Activism in the Lawrence Strike of 1912," in *Women, Work and Protest: A Century of U.S. Women's Labor History*, ed. Ruth Milkman, pp. 42–61 (Boston: Routledge and Kegan Paul, 1985); Karen M. Mason, "Feeling the Pinch: The Kalamazoo Corsetmakers' Strike of 1912," in Groneman and Norton, "*To Toil the Livelong Day*," pp. 141–60; Joan M. Jensen and Sue Davidson, eds., *A Needle, A Bobbin, A Strike: Women Needleworkers in America* (Philadelphia: Temple University Press, 1984): chapters by Joan M. Jensen, "The Great Uprising in Rochester," pp. 94–113; N. Sue Weiler, "The Uprising in Chicago: The Men's Garment Workers Strike, 1910–1911," pp. 114–39; Lois Scharf, "The Great Uprising in Cleveland: When Sisterhood Failed," pp. 146–66; Ann Schofield, "The Uprising of the 20,000: The Making of a Labor Legend," pp. 167–82. See also Meredith Tax, *The Rising of the Women: Feminist Solidarity and Class Conflict, 1880–1917* (New York: Monthly Review Press, 1980); Robin Miller Jacoby, "The Women's Trade Union League and American Feminism," *Feminist Studies* 3 (Fall 1975): 126–40; Nancy Schrom Dye, *As Sisters and as Equals: Feminism, Unionism and the Women's Trade Union League of New York* (Columbia: University of Missouri Press, 1980); and Sarah Eisenstein, *Give Us Bread but Give Us Roses: Working Women's Consciousness in the United States, 1890 to the First World War* (London: Routledge and Kegan Paul, 1983). Three articles by Alice Kessler-Harris lay out many of the issues later pursued in this field: "Where are the Organized Women Workers?" *Feminist Studies* 3 (Fall 1975): 92–110; "Organizing the Unorganizable: Three Jewish Women and Their Union," *Labor History* 17 (Winter 1976): 5–23; and "Stratifying by Sex: Understanding the History of Working Women," in *Labor Market Segmentation*, ed. Richard C. Edwards, Michael Reich, and David M. Gordon, pp. 217–42 (Lexington, Mass.: D.C. Heath, 1975).

77. Martha May, "The Historical Problem of the Family Wage: The Ford Motor Company and the Five Dollar Day," *Feminist Studies* 8 (Summer 1982): 399–424, and "Bread before Roses: American Workingmen, Labor Unions and the Family Wage," in Milkman, *Women, Work, and Protest*, pp. 1–21; Alice Kessler-Harris, *A Woman's Wage: Symbolic Meanings and Social Consequences* (Lexington: University Press of Kentucky, 1990).

78. Goldin, *Understanding the Gender Gap*, quote on p. 66. See also Ileen DeVault, "'Give the Boys a Trade': Gender and Job Choice in the 1890s," in Baron, *Work Engendered*, pp. 191–215, who shows that in the first decades of this century, men's clerical jobs in Pittsburgh were characterized more by respectability and stability than by exceptional possibilities for advancement; and Joanne Meyerowitz, *Women Adrift: Independent Wage Earners in Chicago, 1880–1930* (Chicago: University of Chicago Press, 1988), who discusses the individual and collective strategies by which working women made their own independence viable.

79. Cindy Sondik Aron, *Ladies and Gentlemen of the Civil Service: Middle-Class Workers in Victorian America* (New York: Oxford University Press, 1987); Margery W. Davies, "Women's Place Is at the Typewriter: The Feminization of the Clerical Labor Force," in Edwards, Reich, and Gordon, *Labor Market Segmentation*; and Margery W. Davies, *Women's Place Is at the Typewriter: Office Work and Office Workers, 1870–1930* (Philadelphia: Temple University Press, 1982); Cohen, *From Workshop to Office*; Susan Porter Benson, *Counter Cultures: Saleswomen, Managers, and Customers in American Department Stores, 1890–1940* (Urbana: University of Illinois Press, 1986). Kleinberg's Pittsburgh study shows that these jobs increased even in a primarily heavy industrial city.

80. Nancy F. Cott, *The Bonds of Womanhood: 'Woman's Sphere' in New England, 1780–1835* (New Haven: Yale University Press, 1977); Mary P. Ryan, *Cradle of the Middle Class: The Family in Oneida County, New York, 1780–1865* (Cambridge, England: Cambridge University Press, 1981); Nancy A. Hewitt, *Women's Activism and Social Change: Rochester, N.Y., 1822–1872* (Ithaca, N.Y.: Cornell University Press, 1984); and Hewitt, "Varieties of Voluntarism." See also Lori D. Ginzberg, *Women and the Work of Benevolence: Morality and Politics in the Northeastern United States, 1820–1855* (New Haven: Yale University Press, 1990).

81. Steven M. Buechler, *The Transformation of the Woman Suffrage Movement: The Case of Illinois, 1850–1920* (New Brunswick, N.J.: Rutgers University Press, 1986); Suzanne Lebsock, "Women and American Politics, 1880–1920," in Tilly and Gurin, *Women, Politics, and Change*, pp. 35–62. In the same volume, see the following: Jacqueline Jones, "The Political Implications of Black and White Women's Work in the South, 1890–1965," pp. 108–29; Nancy F. Cott, "Across the Great Divide: Women in Politics Before and After 1920," pp. 153–76; Evelyn Brooks Higginbotham, "In Politics to Stay: Black Women Leaders and Party Politics in the 1920s," pp. 199–220. On women's political mobilization via their role as managers of household budgets, see Dana Frank, "Housewives, Socialists and the Politics of Food: The New York Cost of Living Protests," *Feminist Studies* 11 (1985): 255–85.

82. See Henry Rosovsky, *Capital Formation in Japan, 1868–1940* (New York: Free Press of Glencoe, 1961); Thomas C. Smith, *The Agrarian Origins of Modern Japan* (Stanford, Calif.: Stanford University Press, 1959); John W. Hall, "The Castle Town and Japan's Modern Urbanization," *Far Eastern Quarterly* 15 (November 1955).

83. Laurel Cornell, "Hajnal and the Household in Asia: A Comparativist History of the Family in Preindustrial Japan, 1600–1870," *Journal of Family History* 12 (1987): 143–62, and "Peasant Women and Divorce in Preindustrial Japan," *Signs: Journal of Women in Culture and Society* 15 (1990): 710–32. See also Laurel Cornell, "The Deaths of Old Women. Folklore and Differential Mortality in Nineteenth-Century Japan," in *Recreating Japanese Women, 1600–1945*, ed. Gail Lee Bernstein, pp. 71–87 (Berkeley: University of California Press, 1991), which shows that there is little evidence of gerentocide but abundant suggestion of differential mortality among women; the important variables positively related to female early death were widowhood, being an outsider marrying in, or being without a family. G. William Skinner of the Anthropology Department, University of California, Davis, has looked at infanticide, reproductive strategies, and gender and power within couples

64

as part of his comparative study of several cities and their regions in late Tokugawa Japan. See also Kathleen S. Uno, "Women and Changes in the Household Division of Labor," in Bernstein, *Recreating Japanese Women*, pp. 17–41, who describes considerable flexibility in the household division of labor in the Tokugawa period (varying by class, with the samurai class least flexible, peasants and merchants more so), which disappeared with the spatial separation of work and family in industrialization and the Meiji redefinition of women's place.

84. Laurel Cornell, "Why Are There No Spinsters in Japan?" *Journal of Family History* 9 (1984): 326–39; Robert J. Smith and Ella Lury Wiswell, *The Women of Suye Mura* (Chicago: University of Chicago Press, 1982). Gail Lee Bernstein, *Haruko's World: A Japanese Farm Woman and Her Community* (Stanford, Calif.: Stanford University Press, 1983), shows similar practices persisted in the 1940s and 1950s. For insights into the experience of women in wealthy peasant families, see Anne Walthall, "The Life Cycle of Farm Women in Tokugawa Japan," in Bernstein, *Recreating Japanese Women*, pp. 42–70. An earlier collection of useful essays on Japanese women is Joyce Lebra, Joy Paulson, and Elizabeth Powers, eds., *Women in Changing Japan* (Stanford, Calif.: Stanford University Press, 1976).

85. Gary Saxonhouse and Gavin Wright, "Two Forms of Cheap Labor in Textile History," in *Technique, Spirit and Form in the Making of the Modern Economies: Essays in Honor of William N. Parker*, ed. Gary Saxonhouse and Gavin Wright, pp. 3–31, *Research in Economic History*, Supplement 3 (Greenwich, Conn.: JAI Press, 1984).

86. Gary Saxonhouse, "Country Girls and Communication among Competitors in the Japanese Cotton-Spinning Industry," pp. 97–125 in *Japanese Industrialization and Its Social Consequences*, ed. Hugh Patrick, pp. 97–125 (Berkeley: University of California Press, 1976).

87. Patricia Tsurumi, "Female Textile Workers and the Failure of Early Trade Unionism in Japan," *History Workshop Journal* 18 (Autumn 1984): 3–27, and *Factory Girls: Women in the Thread Mills of Meiji Japan* (Princeton: Princeton University Press, 1990).

88. Barbara Molony, "Activism among Women in the Taisho Cotton Textile Industry," in Bernstein, *Recreating Japanese Women*, pp. 217–38. See also Saxonhouse and Wright, "Two Forms of Cheap Labor."

89. Gail Lee Bernstein, "Women in the Silk-reeling Industry in Nineteenth-Century Japan," in *Japan and the World: Essays on Japanese History and Politics in Honour of Ishida Takeshi*, ed. Gail Lee Bernstein and Haruhiro Fukui, pp. 54–87 (New York: St. Martin's Press, 1988).

90. Joyce Chapman Lebra, "Women in an All-Male Industry: The Case of Sake Brewer Tatsu'uma Kiyo," in Bernstein, *Recreating Japanese Women*, pp. 131–48.

91. Sharon L. Sievers, "Feminist Criticism in Japanese Politics in the 1880s: The Experience of Kishida Toshiko," *Signs: Journal of Women in Culture and Society* 6 (1981): 602–16, and *Flowers in Salt: The Beginnings of Feminist Consciousness in Modern Japan* (Stanford, Calif.: Stanford University Press, 1983); Sharon N. Nolte and Sally Ann Hastings, "The Meiji State's Policy Toward Women, 1890–1910," in Bernstein, *Recreating Japanese Women*, pp. 151–74.

92. Margit Nagy, "Middle-Class Working Women during the Interwar Years," in Bernstein, *Recreating Japanese Women*, pp. 199–216. See also Miriam Silverberg, "The Modern Girl as Militant," ibid., pp. 239–66.

93. Yoshiko Miyake, "Doubling Expectations: Motherhood and Women's Factory Work under State Management in Japan in the 1930s and 1940s," in Bernstein, *Recreating Japanese Women*, pp. 267–95; and Larry S. Carney and Charlotte G. O'Kelly, "Women's Work and Women's Place in the Japanese Economic Miracle," in *Women Workers in Global Restructuring*, ed. Kathryn Ward, pp. 113–45 (Ithaca, N.Y.: ILR Press, Cornell University, 1990).

94. The topic of women in economic development in the contemporary world is one that logically should close this study. Since the early 1970s, much research has been done in this area, following up and going beyond the early analyses of Ester Boserup, *Woman's Role in Economic Development* (London: Allen and Unwin, 1970). Balanced coverage of this experience proved impossible within the length limitations with which I was working. Studies that look comparatively at women in late-industrializing and nonindustrial Asia, the Middle East, Africa, and Latin America, past and present, include Janet Z. Giele and Audrey Smock, eds., *Women and Society in International and Comparative Perspective* (New York: Wiley, 1977); Lois Beck and Nikki Keddie, eds., *Women in the Muslim World* (Cambridge, Mass.: Harvard University Press, 1978); Barbara Rogers, *The Domestication of Women: Discrimination in Developing Societies* (New York: St. Martin's Press, 1979); Lourdes Beneria and Gita Sen, "Accumulation, Reproduction, and Women's Role in Economic Development: Boserup Revisited," *Signs: Journal of Women in Culture and Society* 7 (1981): 279–98; Naomi Black and Ann Baker Cottrell, *Women and World Change: Equity Issues in Development* (Beverly Hills: Sage, 1981); Kate Young, Carol Wolkowitz, and Roslyn McCullagh, eds., *Of Marriage and the Market: Women's Subordination in International Perspective* (London: CSE Books, 1981); Richard Anker, Mayra Buvinic and Nadia H. Youssef, eds., *Women's Roles and Population Trends in the Third World* (London: Croom Helm, 1982); June Nash and Maria Patricia Fernandez-Kelly, eds., *Women, Men and the International Division of Labor* (Albany: SUNY Press, 1984); Daisy Dwyer and Judith Bruce, eds., *A Home Divided: Women and Income in the Third World* (Stanford, Calif.: Stanford University Press, 1988); Susan Tiano, "Gender, Work, and World Capitalism: Third World Women's Role in Development," in *Analyzing Gender*, ed. Beth Hess and Myra Marx Ferree (Beverly Hills: Sage, 1987); Valentine M. Moghadam, *Gender, Development, and Policy: Toward Equity and Empowerment* (Helsinki: World Institute for Development Economics Research [WIDER], 1990); Irene Tinker, ed., *Persistent Inequalities: Women and World Development* (New York: Oxford University Press, 1990); Nikki Keddie and Beth Baron, eds., *Shifting Boundaries: Women and Gender in Middle Eastern History and Theory* (New Haven: Yale University Press, 1991); Nancy Folbre, Bina Agarwal, Maria Floro, and Barbara Bergman, eds., *Women and Work in the World Economy* (London: Macmillan, 1991); and Hilda Kahne and Janet Giele, ed., *Women's Work and Women's Lives: The Continuing Struggle Worldwide* (Boulder, Colo.: Westview Press, 1992). This list includes only comparative studies; there are also many that are country specific.

95. John K. Fairbank, *The Great Chinese Revolution: 1800–1985* (New York:

Harper & Row, 1986), a survey for general readers based on vols. 10 to 15 of the *The Cambridge History of China*, which he helped edit, is the source of the following overview of Chinese political history.

96. Foot binding was much less common in southern China, where women were important workers in household-based rice production, and the Manchus eschewed it altogether. For a firsthand description of the painful process, see Ida Pruitt, *A Daughter of Han: The Autobiography of a Chinese Working Woman* (Stanford, Calif.: Stanford University Press, 1967; originally published 1945), p. 22.

97. Albert Feuerwerker, *China's Early Industrialization: Sheng Hsuan-Huai (1844–1916) and Mandarin Enterprise* (Cambridge, Mass.: Harvard University Press, 1958), quote on p. 16.

98. Thomas G. Rawski, *Economic Growth in Prewar China* (Berkeley: University of California Press, 1989). See also Albert Feuerwerker, *Economic Trends in the Republic of China, 1912–1949*, #31 of Michigan Papers in Chinese Studies (Ann Arbor: Center for Chinese Studies, University of Michigan, 1977). Looking back at economic developments from 1912 to 1949, Rawski argues that despite much disorder, the Chinese economy overall grew at a respectable rate from the end of the World War I to 1937, permitting the population to increase consumption modestly as well as to reproduce itself. Both manufacturing and transportation sectors made substantial gains. There was neither economic collapse nor industrial transformation. Republican governments did not tax agriculture for industrial investment, as did Japan, but the absence of rural reform (of inequal landholding, absentee landlordism, usurious rents, and an inequitable tax system) laid the groundwork for peasant support of the Communist party and its revolution. Both urban and rural economies had collapsed completely by mid-1948.

99. See Dorothy J. Solinger, *From Lathes to Looms: China's Industrial Policy in Comparative Perspective, 1979–1982* (Stanford, Calif.: Stanford University Press, 1991).

100. Most of these examples appear in Ono Kazuko, *Chinese Women in a Century of Revolution: 1850–1950*, ed. Joshua A. Fogel and trans. from Japanese by him and others (Stanford, Calif.: Stanford University Press, 1989; originally published 1978). Yazuko is a Japanese historian of Ming and Qing China who became interested in the modern period and in women's history in the late 1960s, taught courses and gave lectures, and finally wrote this book. Articles published by American scholars that touch the same subjects include Roxane Witke, "Mao Tse-tung, Women and Suicide," and "Woman as Politician in China of the 1920s" (includes Xiang Jingyu); and Suzette Leith, "Chinese Women in the Early Communist Movement" (also discusses Xiang Jingyu), all in *Women in China*, ed. Marilyn B. Young, #15 of Michigan Papers in Chinese Studies (Ann Arbor: Chinese Studies Center, University of Michigan, 1973); and Mary Backus Rankin, "The Emergence of Women at the End of the Ch'ing: The Case of Ch'iu Chin," Marjorie Topley, "Marriage Resistance in Rural Kwangtung," Margery Wolf, "Women and Suicide in China," Yi-Tsi Feuerwerker, "Women as Writers in the 1920's and 1930's," all in *Women in Chinese Society*, ed. Margery Wolf and Roxane Witke (Stanford, Calif.: Stanford University Press, 1975). Janice Stockard, *Daughters of the Canton Delta: Marriage Patterns and Economic Strategies in South China* (Stanford, Calif.:

Stanford University Press, 1989), is the most recent discussion of the "bridedaughters" of Kwangtung and their silk-reeling wage work.

101. Emily Honig, *Sisters and Strangers: Women in the Shanghai Cotton Mills, 1919–1949* (Stanford, Calif.: Stanford University Press, 1986). Another example: Christina Gilmartin, "Gender, Politics, and Patriarchy in China: The Experiences of Early Women Communists, 1920–27," in *Promissory Notes: Women in the Transition to Socialism*, ed. Sonia Kruks, Rayna Rapp, and Marilyn Young, pp. 82–105 (New York: Monthly Review Press, 1989).

102. Arthur P. Wolf, "The Women of Hai-shan: A Demographic Portrait," in Wolf and Witke, *Women in Chinese Society*.

103. Susan Mann, "Grooming a Daughter for Marriage: Brides and Wives in the Mid-Ch'ing Period," pp. 204–30; Rubie S. Watson, "Wives, Concubines, and Maids: Servitude and Kinship in the Hong Kong Region, 1900–1940," pp. 231–55; and Gail Hershatter, "Prostitution and the Market in Women in Early Twentieth-Century Shanghai," pp. 256–85—all in *Marriage and Inequality in Chinese Society*, ed. Rubie S. Watson and Patricia Buckley Ebrey (Berkeley: University of California Press, 1991). In the same volume, see also Patricia Buckley Ebrey, "Introduction," pp. 1–24, and Rubie S. Watson, "Afterword: Marriage and Gender Inequality," pp. 347–68, both of which put the volume's empirical studies into theoretical and comparative frameworks. See also Delia Davin, *Woman-Work: Women and the Party in Revolutionary China* (Oxford, England: Clarendon Press, 1976), which examines marriage and the family in the context of women in the Jiangxi Soviet and liberated areas (i.e., places where Communists were able to institute policies before the declaration of the PRC in 1949).

104. Davin, *Woman-Work*, pp. 26–30, quote on p. 28.

105. Compare, for example, Aleen Holly and Christine Towne Bransfield, "The Marriage Law: Basis of Change for China's Women," in Lynne B. Iglitzin and Ruth Ross, *Women in the World: A Comparative Study*, pp. 363–73 (Santa Barbara: Clio Books, 1976); with Davin, *Woman-Work*, and Jane Barrett, "Women Hold up Half the Sky," in Young, *Women in China*, pp. 193–200.

106. Judith Stacey, *Patriarchy and Socialist Revolution in China* (Berkeley: University of California Press, 1983); Margery Wolf, *Revolution Postponed: Women in Contemporary China* (Stanford, Calif.: Stanford University Press, 1985); Kay Johnson, *Women, the Family and Peasant Revolution in China* (Chicago: University of Chicago Press, 1983), quote on p. 216. An analysis of interviews with emigrés from mainland China and available statistics done by William L. Parish and Martin F. Whyte, *Village and Family in Contemporary China* (Chicago: University of Chicago Press, 1978), had come to similar conclusions earlier. For more recent evaluation, see Jonathan Ocko, "Women, Property, and Law in the People's Republic of China," in Watson and Ebrey, *Marriage and Inequality*, pp. 213–346, which discusses the retreat from free divorce in the marriage law of 1980 and asks whether "changes in enacted law influence changes in practice or merely reflect changes in social and economic organization" (p. 358). On the possibility that village collectivism may again be encouraging patrilocal marriage, see William Lavely, "Marriage and Mobility under Rural Collectivism," in Watson and Ebrey, *Marriage and Inequality in Chinese Society*, pp. 286–312. And for the current views of early commentators,

see Marilyn B. Young, "Chicken Little in China: Women after the Cultural Revolution," pp. 233–47, and Delia Davin, "Of Dogma, Dicta and Washing Machines: Women in the People's Republic of China," pp. 354–58, both in Kruks, Rapp, and Young, *Promisory Notes*.

107. Ansley J. Coale, Wang Feng, Nancy E. Riley, and Lin Fu De, "Recent Trends in Fertility and Nuptiality in China," *Science* 251 (January 26, 1991): 389–93. The 1963 peak was caused by a mini baby boom after the country's recovery from the famine of the GLF and the lingering malnutrition of the following years. In the years from 1940 through 1958, the total fertility rate had ranged from 5 to 6.5 only. See Janet Banister, *China's Changing Population* (Stanford, Calif.: Stanford University Press, 1987), p. 230, table 8.2.

108. Lillian Li, "Life and Death in a Chinese Famine," and James Lee, Cameron Campbell, and Guofu Tan, "Infanticide and Family Planning in Late Imperial China: Price and Population History in Rural Fengtian, 1772–1873," in *Chinese History in Economic Perspective*, ed. Thomas G. Rawski and Lillian M. Li (Berkeley: University of California Press, 1992).

109. Amartya Sen, "More than 100 Million Women Are Missing," *New York Review of Books* 37 (December 20, 1991): 61–66, and unsigned article in the *New York Times* (West Coast ed.), Tuesday, November 5, 1991, pp. B5, B9. See also Ansley Coale, "Excess Female Mortality and the Balance of the Sexes in the Population: An Estimate of the Number of 'Missing Females'" *Population and Development Review* 17 (September 1991): 517–23.

110. Emily Honig and Gail Hershatter, *Personal Voices: Chinese Women in the 1980s* (Stanford, Calif.: Stanford University Press, 1988), acknowledge the urban bias of their sources (magazines addressed to women, advice books for the young, letters to newspapers); only around 30 percent of China's population is urban. Quote is on p. 340.